# *Southern Holiday Lines*

## *in*

# Hampshire

## *and*

# Isle of Wight

# *Alan Bennett*

Published by
**Runpast Publishing**
10 Kingscote Grove, Cheltenham, Glos. GL51 6JX

*To my wife Josephine*

© Alan Bennett,
Runpast Publishing
September 1994

ISBN 1 870754 31 X

Printed by Amadeus Press Ltd
Huddersfield, West Yorkshire
Typesetting by Highlight Type Bureau Ltd
Shipley, West Yorkshire

'Going South for Sunshine, Sonny?' The original composition from which the Southern launched one of their most successful publicity features. Fireman Woolf, of Nine Elms, and the boy, Ronald Witt, were captured, many would say, immortalised, by the child's father who submitted the photograph to Southern Public Relations – the famous poster followed, not to mention the LNER's stylised 'adaptation'. Ronald Witt's family were actually emigrating to California so there was a somewhat longer journey involved than that to the Sunny South Coast! For the record, the locomotive was a 'King Arthur'.

*R.C. Riley collection*

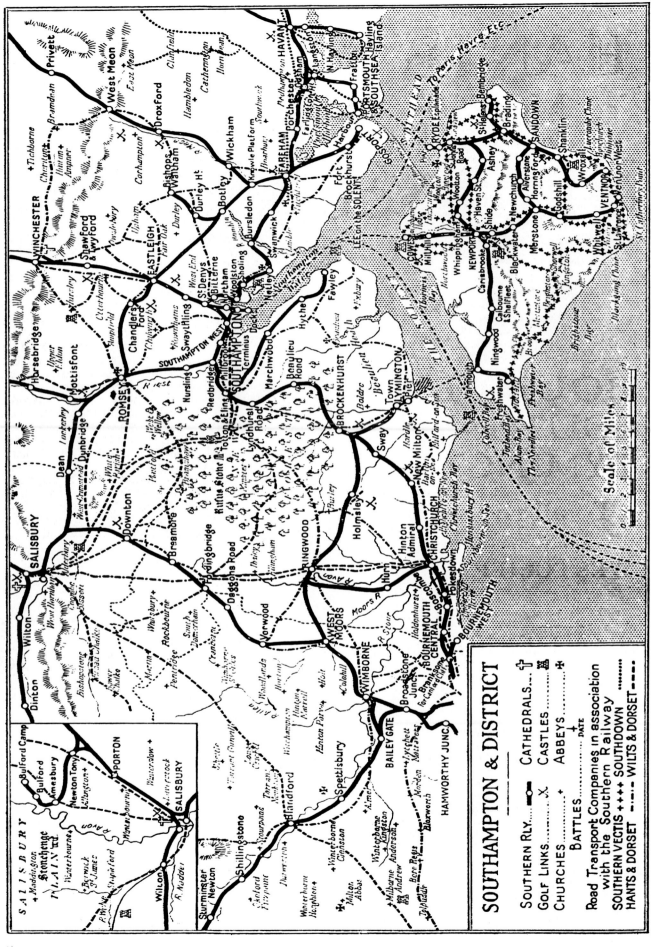

SOUTHAMPTON & DISTRICT

4

# Introduction

The purpose of this book has been two-fold. Primarily, I set out to tell the story of the growth of the South Coast resorts from Portsmouth and Southsea westward through the Solent and New Forest district to Bournemouth and to Poole. Obviously the Isle of Wight would feature prominently in any such work on travel and tourism within this part of Britain overall; likewise there is reference to Weymouth and East Dorset in terms of regional railway/commercial development with regard to essential historical, geographical and structural growth.

Whilst telling the story of the railway and the various resorts defining the region, I also became interested and aware of the range and number of train services serving this South Coast location. Bournemouth, in particular, together with its West Country rival, Torquay, gradually emerged, not only as a stylish regional resort but as a truly national destination, enjoying prestige and a reputation of national proportions. Very few other resorts could claim such an identity. With this in mind, I have incorporated the related theme of what might be called "getting the people there".

Looking at the timetable structure from any time this century, and, especially, the post 1945 to mid 1960s period, one cannot but be aware of the rich diversity of services linking this South Coast district, notably Bournemouth, with the Midlands, the North-West and North-East, South Wales and the West Country, too. Such a range of services, not forgetting, of course, the intense pattern of workings to Portsmouth for the Isle of Wight, and to Bournemouth itself, on the Southern's main lines in and out of Waterloo, represented a significant achievement and a noted acclaim both for the railways and the imagery of the various resorts themselves. Thus it is important here to record details in words, illustrations (these especially so) and in timetable format of the pattern and extent of the railway system

making this South Coast location the undisputed success that it was. We are, therefore, into extensive inter-regional/railway working, bringing in the old pre-grouping companies and later identities of the 'Big Four' after the amalgamations/rationalisations of 1921 and 1948.

Given the overall theme of 'holiday lines' the book has not entered into detailed histories of all the lines eventually leading to that "Sunny South" but there is no apology and, hopefully, sufficient reasoning and explanation, to have included the number of scenes and references to trains and locations far beyond official 'Southern' territory. Hence, *The Pines Express* in Birmingham or locations on the Somerset and Dorset; services over the ex Great Central or the system in the West Midlands, for example. All such references have direct Southern association – Manchester, York, Sheffield, Birkenhead, Bristol etc are all part of the story. The LMS in particular were more than aware of this and of their potential and practice of reaching out in truly national perspectives. Their principal publicity work: "Holidays By LMS" was very different in focus and format from the other three companies. Wherever possible, the original promotional holiday literature has been included here, hopefully adding substance to the overall theme.

One definitive aspect of Southern/LSWR enterprise linked inextricably with this part of the South Coast, namely, traffic and trade through Southampton Docks has not been included here. Thematically and otherwise, this would demand specialist treatment – a book in itself. In related terms the earlier pattern of services – through coaches/connections etc over the former Midland and South Western Junction Railway to and from Southampton are acknowledged but not developed here. For the rest, take the Southern's advice and, hopefully, in the experience of the book: 'Go South For Sunshine!'

## Contents

## Acknowledgements

As ever there are many people to recognise and thank for their contributions to this project.

Don Steggles, Librarian at the Railway Studies Library, Newton Abbot, has been instrumental to the development of the book. The Library is an undoubted centre of excellence and will reward anyone even remotely interested in matters of railway research. I would also thank Terry Knight on behalf of the staff at the Cornish Studies Library, Redruth, for the continued support, going back some ten years now, for this and all my previous projects. Inter-library loans have been invaluable. The active support of the Penzance Subscription Library, another institution well worth sampling, has also been greatly appreciated, giving me access to source materials, otherwise difficult to obtain.

With regard to the photographs, I must again thank R.C. Riley, not least for his help and advice generally, but for the superb prints in particular. Likewise, Michael Mensing who could not have been more helpful. Special thanks here must also go to Roger Venning and Pursey Short for putting a vast collection of material at my disposal and for their part in getting the project moving, initially.

Two further references: first, to Margaret Barron for typing the manuscript, often at little notice, and in the face of extensive amendments; secondly to Stephen Mourton who, as publisher has always supported my work in every way and put it, literally, into printed form. Long live Runpast!

Finally, I would thank my wife, Josephine, as my chief source of inspiration and continuity. The dedication of this book goes, as always, to her.

Alan Bennett, June 1994

PORTSMOUTH

THE RAILWAY STATION.

THE ILLUSTRATED LONDON NEWS, APRIL 8, 1882.

Portsmouth's Town Station as seen here in 1882. This imposing frontage onto Commercial Road was the work of the LBSCR dating from the opening of the line into the city in 1847. It took until 1906, however, before the interior, platforms and accommodation generally matched the elegance and style of the exterior.

# Chapter One

# TO PORTSMOUTH HARBOUR

**P**ortsmouth and Bournemouth shared definite similarities of circumstance in their early railway development, but in terms of their particular character and history they were very different places. Their shared experience was that of the conspicuous failure of the pioneering railway companies – the London and Southampton (the LSWR from 1839) and the Southampton and Dorchester Railway 1847, to provide anything like a confident and direct presence. Portsmouth was served, initially, by the Gosport branch from Bishopstoke (Eastleigh), requiring that passengers begin or complete their journey by ferry; Bournemouth, too, was avoided by the Southampton and Dorchester, being reached only via a branch to Hamworthy Goods, 1847, and a ferry crossing to Poole and thence by road into Bournemouth itself.

The Gosport branch, although opposed by the Admiralty who favoured direct communication form Portsmouth to London via an eastward route along the West Sussex coast, was opened on 29 November 1841. It was closed five days later, not re-opening until 7 February the following year for passengers, but goods began again on December 20. The reason for this was a heavy fall of earth inside Fareham Tunnel, the immediate area, cuttings and tunnel, being described, by one engineer as having all the consistency of rice pudding! The tunnel was driven through a particular type of clay, which, when dry, was solid as in rock, but, when wet, assumed its pudding consistency. The later cutting, 1906, built to avoid the tunnel was driven through similar ground. A wide, shallow cutting was needed, but proved to be constantly troublesome. Being at the end of a 15$^3/4$ mile branch, itself part of a long and indirect route to London, and with a ferry crossing and the bad psychological start/stop to services, there was little to satisfy the people of Portsmouth. Other links followed soon after.

If Portsmouth and Bournemouth shared the initial experience of indirect railway communication and access across water, they were very sharply contrasted as communities in both character, tradition and size. In 1841, for example, the year of the Gosport branch, Portsmouth had a population of 53,941; it was the city of Nelson and the Navy, a vast and prestigious place soon to be heavily fortified in the event of attempted invasion from Europe. Bournemouth, as such, part of the parish of Holdenhurst, accounted for only 691 people. Poole, the only large community locally, had a population of 6,718 in 1851.

Both communities were also closely linked to the progress and influence of the London and Southampton Railway, authorised on 25 July 1834. The route, via Basingstoke, was adopted in preference to a more direct approach because of the potential that it offered for expansion westward into Berkshire, Wiltshire and the lucrative Bristol area.

The London and Southampton, swiftly renamed the London and South Western Railway, opened to Basingstoke on 10 June 1839. On that same day the 12 mile section form Southampton's temporary terminus at Northam to Winchester was also opened, leaving only the 19 mile section between Winchester and Basingstoke

to be completed. The latter involved heavy engineering through the chalk downs, excavating spectacular cuttings brilliantly engineered by Joseph Locke. Completion of the line was celebrated on 11 May 1840 with London and Southampton now linked by rail.

To survey developments at Portsmouth and at Bournemouth from the overall perspective of tourism, it is important to note the strategic significance of Basingstoke, in terms of long-distance traffic from the Midlands and the North off the Great Western Railway's system, and, of Eastleigh, as the junction for Portsmouth, and Salisbury. Treating the two locations Portsmouth and Bournemouth separately, but looking also to compare and contrast, we can focus, first, on Portsmouth, considering Bournemouth at a later stage.

That the Gosport branch was less than satisfactory was something not difficult to appreciate. A more realistic, but somewhat lengthy, through route to London was made possible in 1847 with the completion of the Brighton and Chichester Railway along the Sussex coast. Passengers now had the choice of a 96$^1/4$ mile journey via Brighton or that of 89$^1/2$ miles over the LSWR to Waterloo, but with the ferry crossing. The final link over the Brighton route from Chichester westward was brought into service on 14 June 1847, across the Portcreek and into the city of Portsmouth itself. Further improvements in this easterly direction came with the Brighton company's shortened route via Arundel, Horsham and Dorking which eventually opened on 1 May 1868. The 'Mid-Sussex Line' cut the distance between London and Portsmouth to 87$^3/4$ miles.

Returning again to the late 1840s, another option was available when the LSWR opened its Fareham-Portcreek Junction line, linking into the triangular junction with the Brighton line to the east of Cosham. Thereafter, it gained entry to Portsmouth on the jointly owned section with the Brighton company. The Fareham line opened on 1 October 1848, thus eliminating the need to resort to a ferry for any through destination to Waterloo. This Portsmouth-Waterloo route amounted to 95$^1/2$ miles, equidistant, therefore, with the 'Brighton' route.

Before referring to the final stage in the link between Waterloo and Portsmouth – the 'Portsmouth Direct Line' – it is useful to note that the Winter of 1848, specifically, November, saw the completion of the system which was later to provide through services between Portsmouth and the Midlands. The GWR line from Reading to Basingstoke opened on 1 November, but to broad gauge dimension. Mixed gauge was provided from 22 December 1856 with the broad gauge rails being removed altogether in April 1869.

With mixed gauge between Reading and Didcot, the way to and from the Midlands was secured. The Oxford-Banbury section was 'mixed' in 1852 and in March 1869, the broad gauge north of Oxford, to Wolverhampton, was removed. Leaping ahead, chronologically, but hopefully sustaining the point thematically, the opening of the Great Central Railway on 9 March 1899 offered many new possibilities for through working from the North of England. The Great Central exemplified all that was expected of a modern railway in terms of engineering, and its link line from Culworth Junction,

The signal box gives our location here – Portsmouth Town Station High Level platforms.  4-4-0 'Schools' Class V No 930 *Radley* enters the station from the Portsmouth Harbour terminus on 5 May 1937.  Note the conductor rail for the 'Portsmouth Electrification' inaugurated in July that year.
*R.C. Riley*

Portsmouth and Southsea Low Level platforms seen here on 3 November 1949.  4-4-0 T9 No. 116 leaves with the stopping service for Southampton at 2.03 pm.
*Pursey Short*

This time with Portsmouth and Southsea station in the background, 'King Arthur' Class N15 4-6-0 No 30747 *Elaine* approaches Somers Bridge on the short but busy section between Portsmouth and Southsea and Fratton stations. 6 July 1951.      *Pursey Short*

The Royal Train conveying H.M. The King from London to Portsmouth to visit U.S. Cruiser *Colombus* at the invitation of *C in C, American Naval Forces, Eastern Atlantic and Mediterranean.* 4-6-0 'Lord Nelson' Class No 30863 *Lord Rodney* takes its train of five Pullman cars through Fratton station on 8 November 1949.      *Pursey Short*

south of Woodford Halse, to the Great Western at Banbury, opened to freight on 1 June, and to passengers on 13 August 1900, provided a vital element in the development of broader, more extensive services between the North Country, the East Midlands and the South Coast. The basis of yet another future cross-country service for Portsmouth was also established in March 1847. Authorised on 4 July 1844 the Eastleigh-Salisbury branch was a difficult line to complete. Serving Chandlers Ford and Romsey the line was 21¾ miles long. The Redbridge and Andover line opened on 6 March 1865, also serving Romsey, thus making through Salisbury-Southampton services possible.

Having pursued something of the story of links with the Midlands and North we can now focus again on Portsmouth itself, and the final link with Waterloo. The 'Portsmouth Direct' line from Waterloo via Woking, Guildford and Petersfield, meeting the Sussex coastline just east of Havant, opened to passengers on 1 January 1859. It was met with considerable opposition from South Coast interests, to the extent that services were forcibly blocked at Havant. Sanity eventually prevailed, and LSWR through services to and from Waterloo began on 24 January 1859, but whereas the Portcreek-Portsmouth section, earlier, was Joint, the Havant-Portcreek line extended running powers. At 74½ miles the 'direct' line was obviously shorter but was very heavily graded with long sections of 1 in 80 between Godalming and Rowland's Castle, together with frequent gradients at 1 in 100. Performance-wise, this line came in to its own with the Portsmouth Electrification in July 1937.

Rounding up, we can say that the railway network serving Portsmouth was established, almost completely, by 1860. The coastal link between Southampton and Portsmouth had to wait until 1889 and was opened in two stages: Southampton-Netley on 5 March 1866 and the final section eastward to Fareham on 2 September 1889.

Other than the short-lived Fratton-East Southsea branch (1¼ miles), active from 2 July 1885 to 8 August 1914, the other main developments at Portsmouth itself were the development at the Town Station and the vital extension from the town itself to the Harbour. Whilst preserving the original imposing frontage, Portsmouth Town was rebuilt for 1906. The former arrangements described in 1904 as "consisting of only two platforms, one an island, and badly lighted, protected and arranged "gave way to a new structure with five low-level platforms, and the high-level, island platform, for through trains". The original Brighton line had first breached the northern defences of the city at Hilsea in 1847, and the further extension into the dockyard area passed through the city's inner defences. Reached from Portsmouth and Southsea's new High Level platform, the line crossed Commercial Road and passed the future sites of the Guildhall (opened in 1890) to the south, and Victoria Park to the north. 'The Illustrated London News' in 1882 recognised that the extension from the town to the Harbour station was a valuable improvement for passengers, but it noted that in crossing Victoria Park on its embankment the railway had divided the park into "two very unequal portions, depriving it of any pretension to an imposing appearance". Carried on a substantial embankment, the line crossed the main road close to Gun Wharf and led into Portsmouth Harbour station, built over the water itself and giving immediate access to the ferries for both the Isle of Wight and the short but busy crossing to Gosport.

The Harbour station opened on 2 October 1876, an obvious improvement in terms of traffic to the Isle of Wight. Prior to this, the alternatives for those visiting the Island was the provision of a horse tramway from Portsmouth Town to Clarence Pier, operating from May 1865, or, indeed, departure from Stokes Bay where a short branch line 1¼ miles off the Gosport branch itself gave direct access to steamers for Ryde. Never a realistic rival for the Portsmouth-Ryde crossing the Stokes Bay service ceased with the onset of World War One. Waterloo-Portsmouth services during the summer season in 1914 are included here.

### WATERLOO – PORTSMOUTH – RYDE SUMMER 1914

**Waterloo dep**

| | | |
|---|---|---|
| 5.15 am | arr Portsmouth Harbour | 7.59 arr Ryde 8.40 am |
| 6.20 am | arr Portsmouth Harbour | 9.26 arr Ryde 10.25 am |
| 6.55 am | arr Portsmouth Harbour | 9.66 arr Ryde 10.55 am |
| 8.55 am | arr Portsmouth Harbour | 11.55 arr Ryde 12.50 pm |
| 9.10 am | arr Portsmouth Harbour | 11.16 arr Ryde 12.00 pm |
| 11.10 am | arr Portsmouth Harbour | 2.00 arr Ryde 2.40 pm |
| 12.46 pm | Luncheon Car Train | 2.43 arr Ryde 3.25 pm |
| 1.17 pm | arr Portsmouth Town | 3.54 arr Ryde 5.15 pm |
| 2.35 pm | arr Portsmouth Harbour | 5.34 arr Ryde 6.40 pm |
| 3.45 pm | arr Portsmouth Harbour | 6.00 arr Ryde 6.40 pm |
| 4.30 pm | arr Portsmouth Harbour | 6.55 arr Ryde 7.40 pm |
| 4.55 pm | arr Portsmouth Harbour | 7.10 arr Ryde 7.50 pm |
| 5.48 pm | arr Portsmouth Town | 8.12 arr Ryde 9.15 pm |
| 6.40 pm | Dining Car Express Portsmouth Harbour | |
| | | 8.36 arr Ryde 9.15 pm |
| 7.10 pm | arr Portsmouth Town | 10.00 arr Ryde 12.00 |
| 10.35 pm | arr Portsmouth Town | 1.05 arr Ryde 3.10 am |

**Ryde/Portsmouth Harbour dep**

6.53 am  dep Portsmouth Town            arr Waterloo 9.34 am
7.05 am  dep Ryde dep Portsmouth Harbour 7.40
                                        arr Waterloo 9.55 am
8.00 am  dep Ryde dep Portsmouth Harbour 8.50
                                        arr Waterloo 11.33 am
8.50 am  dep Ryde  dep Portsmouth Harbour 9.35
                                        arr Waterloo 11.39 am
10.08 am dep Portsmouth Town            arr Waterloo 1.12 pm
10.10 am dep Ryde dep Portsmouth Harbour 11.10
                                        arr Waterloo 2.25 pm
11.15 am dep Ryde dep Portsmouth Harbour 12.00*
                                        arr Waterloo 2.20 pm
1.25 pm  dep Ryde dep Portsmouth Town 2.40
                                        arr Waterloo 4.34 pm
2.00 pm  dep Ryde dep Portsmouth Harbour 2.45
                                        arr Waterloo 4.50 pm
2.00 pm  dep Ryde dep Portsmouth Harbour 3.00
                                        arr Waterloo 6.18 pm
*Luncheon Car Train
5.00 pm dep Ryde dep Portsmouth harbour 5.45pm*
                                        arr Waterloo 8.03 pm
6.00 pm dep Portsmouth Town            arr Waterloo 9.24 pm
6.15 pm dep Ryde dep Portsmouth Harbour 7.00
                                        arr Waterloo 9.06 pm
6.30 pm dep Ryde dep Portsmouth Town 8.00
                                        arr Waterloo 11.02 pm
8.05 pm dep Ryde dep Portsmouth Town 9.08
                                        arr Waterloo 12.04 am

* Dining Car Express

Humbler, more routine duties at Fratton shed as seen in these two excellent interior views. Sunshine, shadow and smoke make for that definitive atmosphere of the steam shed at rest. The U Class 2-6-0 No 31809 is prominent in the photograph from March 1953; the presence of the shed worker completes the view from 1949, with the four locomotives around the turntable. *Pursey Short*

Bedhampton Crossing west of Havant on Sunday 29 May 1947. In a photograph redolent of the period Southern Electric 2 BIL set, No 2105, works westward on a Brighton-Portsmouth service.
*Pursey Short*

Cosham Junction to the west, Farlington Junction to the east, and Portcreek Junction at the south comprised the triangular layout enabling trains to enter and leave Portsmouth to the east or west, or, indeed, avoid it altogether, as seen here. The westbound Brighton-Plymouth approaches Farlington Junction headed by Light Pacific No 21C142 later to become 'West Country' No 34042 *Dorchester*.
*Pursey Short*

Cosham station was to the north of the city across Portcreek. Here the daily Plymouth-Brighton service races through the station behind 'West Country' Class Light Pacific 4-6-2 No 34037 *Clovelly*. 18 June 1949
*Pursey Short*

A Portsmouth-Cardiff service in 1951 sees a 4-4-0 Class L12, No 30433 near the site of the former Paulsgrove Race Course Halt – a thirties development – between Cosham and Portchester on the Fareham line. Opened in June 1933, it closed with the coming of war in 1939.
*Pursey Short*

The fastest 'down' service to Portsmouth Harbour was, inevitably, the Dining Car Express at 1 hour 56 mins; the fastest 'up' service was the corresponding Express at 2 hours 18 mins; By comparison, the *LBSCR's* Mid-Sussex route gave a fastest timing of 2 hours and 3 mins departing Victoria at 11.35 am, arriving Portsmouth Harbour at 1.38 pm, despite a journey of 86½ miles as against the *LSWR's* 74½ miles. The 4.50 pm departure from London Bridge, with slip portions for Bognor and Littlehampton, arrived at Portsmouth Harbour at 7.00 pm, another competitive services by the *LBSCR*.

For the direct Portsmouth line from Waterloo, the third-rail Electrification Scheme, sanctioned under the Railways Agreement Act of 1935, was undoubtedly the most significant influence since its opening many years before. Holiday traffic to Portsmouth and the Isle of Wight had increased substantially during the inter-war years. According to the 'Southern Railway Magazine', more than 971,000 people used the Waterloo-Portsmouth services during 1936 with an average of 16 trains in each direction daily. Electrification would provide a faster service, a greater number of trains and, crucially, a more, progressive image for the Southern Railway. Clean, fast and efficient service was to be the hallmark.

Introduced at an estimated cost of £3,000,000, the new electric service began between Waterloo and Portsmouth Harbour on 4 July 1937. It brought about a transformation. On timetabling, the fastest non-stop service between Waterloo and Portsmouth Harbour was 92 minutes offering significant acceleration, cutting travel time by 20 minutes. Fast trains to Portsmouth left Waterloo at hourly intervals from 7.50 am to 9.50 pm; stopping trains departed at 27 minutes and 57 minutes past the hour. In the 'up' direction, fast trains left Portsmouth Harbour at hourly intervals from 9.20 am to 10.20 pm; stopping services departed from Portsmouth and Southsea on the half hour and the hour. What were termed 'business semi-fasts', five 'up' workings between 7.23 am and 8.42 am, together with three early-evening return services at 4.20 pm, 5.20 pm and 6.20 pm were also provided. Saturday service reflected what Southern publicity called 'The Call of the South'. Responding to demand and anticipating increased traffic, there was lavish provision. The *Railway Gazette* gave details:

On Saturdays in summer the standard service over the Portsmouth direct line is increased by three fast trains an hour in each direction, one of which runs non stop between Waterloo and Portsmouth and Southsea in the 'down' direction and from Portsmouth Harbour to Waterloo in the 'up' direction, thus catering specifically for Isle of Wight passengers. The second calls only at Havant, connecting to Hayling Island; the third only at Guildford and Portsmouth and Southsea; and the fourth makes the normal weekday fast trip with calls at Guildford, Haslemere and Portsmouth and Southsea. The Sunday service is made up as traffic requirements dictate, with a minium increase of one fast train an hour in each direction in the summer, plus special excursions organised by the Southern Railway and the National Sunday League.

Considerable modifications were required to stations and infrastructure generally. Amongst the more notable was Havant station which was completely rebuilt,

Portsmouth and Southsea High Level platforms lengthened to 800 feet, as at Woking, Guildford and Haslemere, and the redevelopment of Portsmouth Harbour for the Isle of Wight traffic. Again, the *Railway Gazette* provides details:

Traffic to the Isle of Wight has developed so rapidly during the last ten years and more that progressive improvements have had to be made at Portsmouth Harbour station in order to cope with it. At the terminal end of the platforms the means of transfer between train and boat are now probably as efficient as it is possible to make them within the limited space available. The work that has had to be done directly in connection with the electrification has been that of extending four of the five platforms to accommodate the new 12-car trains and improve the curvature at the outer ends of the platforms. This has meant some difficult work in widening the approach viaduct and rearranging the permanent way. The fact that the whole of this work was completed far enough to deal with the 20 full-length electric trains for the Naval Review traffic on 20 May without it having been allowed to interfere with normal traffic is typical of the smart work the Southern Railway engineers are now practised in carrying out.

The new Harbour station reflected the change from wood to steel. Built out over the water, the station was supported by a steel foundation, itself secured by steel piles and braces screwed deep into the bed-rock below. As shown here, the new station was not only much more modern in material and design, it was also significantly larger than its less distinguished predecessor, the subject of much criticism in terms of its condition and image by the mid thirties. Whilst the roof section was extended by up to 250 feet to give overall coverage of 650 feet, (platform 2-5 being all in excess of 800 feet) work on the new booking hall, offices, waiting rooms and parcels accommodation was deferred until the Autumn in order to cope effectively with the intense summer traffic for the Isle of Wight. The hip-roofed signal box was sited on the 'up' side immediately beyond platform one and the access to and from the dock-yard line.

From Portsmouth Town station to Fratton a relief line was also brought into use, this being the conversion of a former siding on the 'down' side. Fratton also became the site for the new carriage sheds and cleaning plant provided in connection with the new electrified stock. This shed, one of four in all, was built to standard dimensions 820 feet long and 60 feet wide. Constructed of steel and corrugated asbestos the sheds housed four sets of rails. This, of course, leads to the final reference to this prestigious project by the Southern. Constructed at the Company's Eastleigh Works, the new stock comprised 48 four-coach units 4-COR, 19 of them being fitted with Kitchen-Car, 38 two-coach units, corridored (2-BILS), 8 two-coach units, 6 three-coach units, and 5 two-coach trailer units, these last three categories all being new-corridor stock.

Thus, from the Summer of 1937 Portsmouth and Southsea became part of the Southern Railway's famed 'Electric Coast'. The 'Mid-Sussex', and Coastal lines westward from Worthing, including Bognor and Littlehampton, followed suit under the 'Portsmouth Number Two' project, this becoming operative from 2 July, 1938.

Pushing westward, this time, between Portchester and Fareham, we see a Portsmouth-Southampton service headed by 4-4-0 Class S11 No 30396 on 10 June 1950. Steam working on any regular basis ended on local stopping trains such as these in September 1957 with the introduction of the 'Eastleigh' or Hampshire Units, diesel-electric sets that did much to boost image and trade. *Pursey Short.*

Fareham became an important junction and interchange for a number of locations in this part of Hampshire. Originally the line from Bishopstoke (Eastleigh) to Gosport served the town but its importance as a railway junction grew rapidly thereafter with the expansion of the network. In this first view, 4-4-2 Class H2 No 32421 *South Foreland* enters the station from the east rounding the severe curvature here. The train was a Brighton-Bournemouth working of 1952. Note the original straight alignment to the right of the train – the Gosport branch of 1841 vintage. Fareham West signal box is also seen here. *Pursey Short*

With the declaration of War on that famous Sunday morning of 3 September 1939, Portsmouth became an inevitable target for the Luftwaffe. When air-raids came in the Autumn and Winter of 1940, the city braced itself for an horrific ordeal. The Harbour station was badly damaged by bombs in August 1940, but the night of 10 and 11 January 1941 could never be forgotten. Portsmouth Harbour station was effectively destroyed, the Town station and Fratton were also extensively damaged and symbolically, the Guildhall so close to the Town station, was gutted by incendiaries. Post-war services would require much preparatory work, the Southern's final contribution to the city, prior to Nationalisation. Rebuilding at Portsmouth Harbour was completed in June 1946.

A Portsmouth-Eastleigh train of GWR stock and 4-4-0 Class D15 No 30467 leave Fareham on Sunday 29 May 1949. The fireman reaches for the single line token for the original tunnel route.
*Pursey Short*

At the opposite end of the station in much finer weather we see Fareham East Junction signal box and 4-6-0 'Remembrance' Class No 2327 *Trevithick* leaving the Fareham Tunnel avoiding line with a Reading-Portsmouth train on 5 May 1947. The Southampton line curves away to the left; the tunnel avoiding line opened in 1906 being worked until 1973.
*Pursey Short*

Out into the country north-west of Fareham, the 3.34 pm Sats. Portsmouth-Wolverhampton service heads for Eastleigh hauled by 4-4-0 Class D15 No 30472 on 10 June 1950.
*Pursey Short*

Another Summer Saturday service, this one on the Fareham-Southampton line sees the 2.33 pm Portsmouth-Bristol train, made up from Great Western stock and 2-6-0 U Class No 31795 just to the west of Fareham in an attractive rural setting, 10 June 1950.
*Pursey Short*

It would be difficult not to include one view, at least, of the Hayling Island branch from the main line at Havant. Here we have AIX 0-6-0T No 32677 crossing Langstone Bridge on Sunday 21 August 1949, with a train for the seaside. The locomotive was an ex Isle of Wight representative – W13, *Carisbrooke*. *Pursey Short.*

# Chapter Two
# THE ISLE OF WIGHT – 'THE HOLIDAY ISLE'

Records were broken for holiday travel to the Isle of Wight in 1928. During that year the Portsmouth-Ryde crossing, the principal access to the Island, carried over two million people, the 2,000,000th passenger being counted onto the 11.05 am Ryde-Portsmouth ferry on 14 December. it was also noted that numbers were up by 300,000 on the previous year. Five years later, the August Bank Holiday crowds at Waterloo over the three day weekend numbered over 78,000, many of them bound for Portsmouth and the Isle of Wight. Indeed, the queue for these particular services overflowed the extensive station area itself, reaching some hundred yards or so along the road outside.

These two examples of seasonal travel taken from what became the definitive period of the English seaside holiday, reflect the broad appeal of the Isle of Wight, which, by virtue of its favourable climate and easy accessibility, had also become significant in residential terms. Seductive Southern Railway imagery promoted the various features of 'The Holiday Isle' or 'Garden Isle' so as to meet all requirements.

Of the Island's many resorts, so closely associated with railway development, Ryde was both the largest and the first of its kind. As indicated, it owed much to its proximity to Portsmouth and, therefore, tourist traffic by steamer, but not least, to the progressive response of the town itself, anxious to maximise its potential. By the turn of the century Ryde had consolidated its position as the largest resort, and whilst other island locations, Sandown, Shanklin and Ventnor for example had grown considerably, Ryde sustained a substantially higher population, larger than that of Newport, the administrative and commercial capital and Cowes, the island's chief port in the mid nineteenth century. Population figures for these places in 1901 indicate relative growth:

| | |
|---|---|
| Ryde | 11,042 |
| Newport | 10,911 |
| Cowes | 8,654 |
| Ventnor | 5,866 |
| Sandown | 5,006 |
| Shanklin | 4,533 |

Whilst railway development on the Island itself played no part in the very early growth of Ryde, it was instrumental in terms of the other resorts. In serving Sandown, Shanklin and Ventnor directly from Ryde itself, the Isle of Wight Railway ensured both for itself and for these resorts, the premier position in the tourist market. An outline of railway development on the Island would be useful at this stage.

The first line to open was the Cowes and Newport Railway, authorised on 8 August 1859 and opened on 16 June 1862. This 4¼ mile link between the chief port and the capital town was inevitable, so, too, was that of the Isle of Wight Railway Company with its line from Ryde St. Johns Road to Shanklin and Ventnor, (11¼ miles) authorised on 23 July 1860 and opening to Shanklin on 23 August 1864, and to Ventnor on 10 September 1866. By sacrificing strict chronology for the purpose of greater clarity, it is as well at this stage to record the formation of the Isle of Wight Central Railway in July 1887. This was an amalgam of three somewhat impoverished lines, the

founder member being the Cowes and Newport, then joined by the Isle of Wight and Newport Junction Railway's line from Sandown to Shide, (Incorporated 31 July 1868, and opened on 1 February 1875) thereafter, opening the final mile to Newport, in two stages, completed on 1 June 1879, (9¼ miles) in and, finally, the Ryde and Newport Railway from Smallbrook Junction (linking with the Isle of Wight Company) to Newport, authorised on 25 July 1872 and opening on 20 December 1875 (8 miles). Another line worked by the Isle of Wight Central – the Newport, Godshill and St Lawrence Railway – left the Newport-Sandown line at Merstone, struck south to Ventnor, and, whilst opening to St Lawrence on 20 July 1897, had to wait until 1 June 1900 to complete the 1¼ miles to Ventnor Town, 6¼ miles overall. Merstone, the junction station, was rebuilt in 1897. Formerly a single platform, the new building was an island platform allowing trains to cross en-route.

Although there were now two routes into Ryde, from Ventnor and from Newport, the railhead at Ryde was someway into the town at St John's Road. Communication between ships at Ryde Pier and the station at St John's, 1¼ miles distant, was provided by a horse-drawn train service, initially, along the pier from 29 August 1864 and, eventually, to St John's on 1 August 1871. As with a somewhat familiar situation in Portsmouth with the link to and from Clarence Pier, this access was not seen to be satisfactory. A much improved facility was opened jointly by the London Brighton and South Coast, and London and South Western Railways on 12 July 1880. First authorised on 23 July 1877 the new railway link offering direct services to and from the steamers opened to Ryde Esplanade on 5 April 1880 and to Ryde Pier Head station three months later on 12 July. The line was worked by the two Island companies.

Two further lines completed the network. First was the short 2¾ mile branch from Brading on the Isle of Wight Railway to Bembridge opening on 27 May 1882; steamer traffic was encouraged here for a short time after opening. Initially the property of the Brading Harbour Railway, the line eventually passed to the Isle of Wight Company (who had always worked it) in 1898. Finally, three was the Freshwater, Yarmouth and Newport Railway, at 12 miles opening up the beautiful 'Western Wight'. Authorised on 26 August 1880, the line opened to traffic on 20 July 1889.

Under the Grouping, of course, the Island's railways passed into the ownership of the newly formed Southern Railway from 1 January 1923, or almost so. In fact, the Freshwater, Yarmouth and Newport did not enter the fold until 1 August that year, its prospects being seen by the Southern as something less than commercially desirable. Of the various lines, the Isle of Wight Central was the most extensive, serving in its final form the important towns of Cowes, Ryde, Sandown and Ventnor, making up a substantial system with Newport as the hub. But if the Isle of Wight Central was the most extensive then the Isle of Wight Railway with Sandown, Shanklin and Ventnor in its possession was, inevitably, the most prosperous.

The London and Southern Western Railway timetable for the Summer Season 1914 carried a useful summary

# LONDON & THE ISLE OF WIGHT

## BY THREE ROUTES.

| DOWN. | | WEEK DAYS. |
|---|---|---|

| | | a.m. | a.m. | a.m. | a.m. | | a.m. | a.m. | a.m. | a.m. | a.m. | a.m. | | p.m. | p.m. | p.m. | p.m. | p.m. | | p.m. | p.m. |
|---|---|---|---|---|---|---|---|---|---|---|---|---|---|---|---|---|---|---|---|---|---|
| **LONDON (Waterloo)** dep. | | 5 15 | 5 35 | 5 50 | | 6 10 | | 6 20 | 7 40 | 6A55 | 9 10 | 1015 | 10 15 | | 1140 | 12 30 | 1245 | 12 40 | 1250 | | 1 17 | 2 20 |
| Ryde Pier arr. | | 8 40 | | | | | | 10 25 | | 10A55 | 12 0 | | | | | 3 25 | | | 5 15 | | 5 45 |
| Sandown | | 9 40 | | | | | | 11 9 | | | 1945 | | 2 26 | | | 4 10 | | | 5 50 | | 6 21 |
| Shanklin | | 9 46 | | | | | | 11 15 | | | 1251 | | 2 34 | | | 4 22 | | | 5 55 | | 6 27 |
| **VENTNOR (I.W.R.)** | | 10 0 | | | | | | 11 30 | | | 1 0 | | 2 50 | | | 4 35 | | | 6 8 | | 6 40 |
| COWES | | | 9 15 | | | | | 11 40 | 12 5 | | 20 | | 3 25 | | 5 0 | 4 45 | | 4 45 | | | 6 55 |
| Newport | | | 1012 | | | | | 11 30 | 1253 | | 1253 | | 3 47 | | 5 12 | | | | | | 6 29 |
| Sandown | | | 1048 | | | | | | 1 33 | | | | | 4 22 | | | | | | |
| **VENTNOR TN. (I.W.C.)** | | | 1051 | | | | | | | | | | | | | 3 30 | | 3 40 | 5 55 | | |
| Yarmouth | | | | 9 20 | | 1115 | | | | | | 1 20 | | | | 3 55 | | | | | 5 20 |
| Freshwater Bay | | | | | | 1150 | | | | | | 1 55 | | | | 4 5 | | | | | 5 5 |
| TOTLAND BAY | | | | 1015 | | 1145 | | | | | | 1 50 | | | | 4 0 | | 4 10 | | | 5 50 |
| ALUM BAY | | | | | | 12 0 | | | | | | | | | | 4 15 | | 4 25 | | | |

| DOWN. | | WEEK DAYS—continued. | | | | | | | | | SUNDAYS. |
|---|---|---|---|---|---|---|---|---|---|---|---|

| | | p.m. | p.m. | p.m. | p.m. | p.m. | p.m. | p.m. | p.m. | | | a.m. | a.m. | a.m. | a.m. | a.m. | a.m. | noon | p.m. | p.m. | p.m. | p.m. |
|---|---|---|---|---|---|---|---|---|---|---|---|---|---|---|---|---|---|---|---|---|---|---|
| **LONDON (Waterloo)** dep. | | 2 55 | 3 45 | 4 30 | 4 50 | 4 55 | 6 0 | 6H40 | 7810 | 1035 | | 8630 | 9 20 | 9 35 | 10 5 | 10 | 1150 | 12 0 | 2030 | 5 25 | 5 45 | 1040 |
| Ryde Pier arr. | | 6 40 | 7 40 | | | 7650 | | 9H15 | 12s 0 | 3 10 | | 12320 | 12 45 | 2 45 | | | | | 6s10 | 8 40 | | 3 10 |
| Sandown | | 7 12 | | | | 8 22 | | 9u51 | 8c20 | | | | 1 30 | 3 27 | | | | | 8s 5 | 9 10 | | 8 25 |
| Shanklin | | 7 18 | | | | 8 27 | | 9u56 | 8c53 | | | | 1 35 | 3 33 | | | | | 8c10 | 9 16 | | 8 33 |
| **VENTNOR (I.W.R.)** | | 7 32 | | | | 8 40 | | 10u10 | 8c46 | | | | 1 47 | 3 50 | | | | | 8c23 | 9 30 | 9 55 | 8 46 |
| COWES | | 6 55 | | | | 9 20 | 10 | 10u15 | | | | | 1 55 | 3 50 | | 3 40 | | | | 9 55 | 10 17 | 9 23 |
| Newport | | 7 27 | | | | 9 40 | 10 37 | 9u55 | 12r31 | | | 1 36 | | 4 12 | | 4 28 | | | | 9 31 | 10 7 | 9 50 |
| Sandown | | 8 14 | | | | | | | | | | | | 4 46 | | | | | | | | |
| **VENTNOR TN. (I.W.C.)** | | 8 17 | | | 7 55 | | | | | | | | | 3 52 | | | | | | | | |
| Yarmouth | | | | | | | | | | | | 1 10 | | | | 1 10 | | 3 5 | | | | |
| Freshwater Bay | | | | | 8 20 | | | | | | | | | | | | | | | | | |
| TOTLAND BAY | | | | | | | | | | | | 1 40 | | | | 1 40 | | 3 35 | | | | |
| ALUM BAY | | | | | | | | | | | | | | | | | | | | | | |

A Saturdays only commencing 4th July.   B Thursdays and Saturdays only.   C On Sunday mornings arrive Sandown 9.50, Shanklin 9.55 and Ventnor 10.8 a.m.   D During June arrive 7.55 p.m.   G July, August and September only.   H Thursdays, Fridays and Saturdays only during June and every Week-day commencing 1st July.   L Arrive Ryde 8.45 p.m. during June.   M These times apply daily 13th July to 12th September, and Thursdays, Fridays and Saturdays only before and after.   P Friday mornings only.   § Three minutes later on Saturdays.

| UP. | | WEEK DAYS. |
|---|---|---|

| | | a.m. | a.m. | a.m. | a.m. | a.m. | | a.m. | | a.m. | a.m. | a.m. | | p.m. | p.m. | p.m. | p.m. | | p.m. | p.m. | p.m. |
|---|---|---|---|---|---|---|---|---|---|---|---|---|---|---|---|---|---|---|---|---|---|
| **ALUM BAY** dep. | | | | | | | | | | | | | | 12 30 | | | | | | | 5 5 |
| TOTLAND BAY | | | | 7 0 | | 8 35 | | | | | | | | 1 5 | | | | | | | 5 30 |
| Freshwater Bay | | | | 7 25 | | 9 0 | | | 9 25 | | | | | 1 20 | | | | | | | 4 50 |
| Yarmouth | | | | | | | | | 1015 | | | | | 1 30 | | | | | | | |
| **VENTNOR TN. (I.W.C.)** | | | | | | 8 22 | | 9 44 | | | | | | 1224 | 12 24 | | | | | | |
| Sandown | | | | | | 9 0 | | 9 47 | | | | | | 1227 | 12 27 | | | | | | |
| Newport | | | 6 45 | 7 35 | | 9 8 | | 1023 | | | | | | 1 10 | 1 30 | | 3 10 | | | 5 20 | |
| COWES | | | 7 15 | 7 10 | | 9 50 | | 10 0 | | | | | | 1240 | 1 30 | | 3 45 | | | 5 30 | |
| **VENTNOR (I.W.R.)** | | 6A30 | | 7s20 | 8 5 | | | 1020 | | | | | | 1 18 | | | | | | | |
| Shanklin | | 6A40 | | 7s30 | 8 18 | | | 1033 | | | | | | 1 25 | | 2 25 | | | | 5 44 | |
| Sandown | | 6A45 | | 7s35 | 8 24 | | | 1040 | | | | | | 1 28 | | 2 25 | | | | 6 16 | |
| Ryde Pier | | 7 M5 | | 8 0 | 8 50 | | | 1115 | | | | | | 1 35 | | 2 40 | | | | | |
| **LONDON (Waterloo)** arr. | | 9 55 | 1120 | 11 33 | 1139 | 12 30 | | 1 31 | | 1 55 | 2 0 | 45 | | 4 46 | 4 50 | 5 | 6 45 | 7 31 | | 7 31 | |

| UP. | | WEEK DAYS—continued. | | | | | | | | | SUNDAYS. |
|---|---|---|---|---|---|---|---|---|---|---|---|

| | | p.m. | p.m. | p.m. | | p.m. | | p.m. | | a.m. | a.m. | p.m. | p.m. | p.m. | p.m. | p.m. | p.m. | p.m. |
|---|---|---|---|---|---|---|---|---|---|---|---|---|---|---|---|---|---|---|---|
| **ALUM BAY** dep. | | | 7 0 | | | D | | | | | | | 2 0 | | | | 6 5 | |
| TOTLAND BAY | | | | | | | | | | | | | | | | | 6 5 | |
| Freshwater Bay | | | | 7 30 | | | | | | | | 1 10 | | | | | 6 25 | |
| Yarmouth | | | 7 30 | | | | | | | | | | | | | | 6 35 | |
| **VENTNOR TN. (I.W.C.)** | | 4 30 | | | | 6 0 | | | | | | | 2068 | 2 58 | | | | |
| Sandown | | 3 55 | | 6 40 | | 8 E 0 | | 8 45 | | | | 4 15 | 4 15 | 3 37 | | | | |
| Newport | | 6 15 | | 7 50 | | | | | 7 30 | 12 0 | | 4 0 | 4 0 | | | | | |
| COWES | | 6 0 | | 6 20 | | 8 15 | | 8 30 | | | | | | | | | | |
| **VENTNOR (I.W.R.)** | | | 6 50 | | | | 8 40 | | 6c55 | | 12r15 | | | | | 6 45 | 6 40 | |
| Shanklin | | | 7 3 | | | | 8 53 | | 7c 6 | | 12r26 | 4 20 | | | | 6 55 | 6 52 | |
| Sandown | | | 7 9 | | | | 8 57 | | 7e11 | | 12r31 | 4 27 | | | | 7 2 | 6 57 | |
| Ryde Pier | | | | 7645 | | | 9 20 | | 7e40 | | 1 H 0 | 4 55 | | | | 7 30 | 9 20 | |
| **LONDON (Waterloo)** arr. | | 10 5 | 12 | 4 12 | 4 | 12 4 | | 3 35 | | 10c41 | 11 4 | 6 35 | 8 36 | 8 6 | 8 48 | 9 37 | 1025 | 8 35 |

A—Mondays only commencing 6th July.   B—Runs every Week-day 3rd August to 12th September (Mondays only before and after).   C July, August and September only.   D—Passengers from the Isle of Wight and Cowes by this boat must find their own way from Southampton Royal Pier to Southampton West Station.   E—Leaves Sandown 7.15 p.m. commencing July.   F—These times apply during July, August and September.   During June leave Sandown 7.15 p.m.   G—Thursdays, Fridays and Saturdays only during June leave Ryde 8.5 p.m.   H Leave Ryde 1.25 p.m. during July.   J—During June leave Newport 3.10 and Cowes at 3.45 p.m.   L—Via Totland Bay.   M—Mondays only during June and every Week-day commencing July.

## TIME TABLES OF OTHER ISLE OF WIGHT SERVICES,

### Including Intermediate Stations, as follows:

| PAGES. | TO AND FROM | ROUTES. |
|---|---|---|
| 56 to 77 | London, Eastleigh, Southampton, Brockenhurst and intermediate stations | via Southampton, Portsmouth and Lymington. |
| 82 to 87 | London, Leatherhead, New Guildford and Portsmouth direct line stations | via Portsmouth. |
| 88 and 91 | Salisbury, Redbridge, Eastleigh, and Netley Line stations | via Portsmouth. |
| 124 and 125 | Great Western stations | via Portsmouth. |

*LSWR* Timetable, 1914

E_42674. RYDE, I.O.W:- THE PIER.

Ryde Esplanade with the Pier Head beyond, the date given for this print being September 1919. Ryde St Johns to the Pier Head was a joint LBSCR/LSWR initiative opening in July 1880. Note the prevailing sense of order, stability and confidence that defines this view.

Comparisons and contrast on the Isle of Wight. The bustle, energy and atmosphere of Ryde Pier Head terminus with the gulls reeling and platforms busy with trains, offers a very different image from that of rural Freshwater, the entire composition being quintessential branch line England.

At Ryde, Pursey Short's photograph sees the remodelled terminus of four platforms in the late season of 1948. O2 Class 0-4-47 W20 *Shanklin* waits at the far platform with a Ventnor train whilst sister locomotive W21 *Sandown* takes water prior to leaving for Newport and Cowes.

*Pursey Short*

R.C. Riley's late summer idyll at Freshwater in September 1953 sees a solitary O2 Class No 33 *Bembridge* at the terminus deserted and peaceful in the sunshine. The atmosphere itself is terminal; time was being called for this branch to the 'Western Wight', as closure came here that same month.

*R.C. Riley*

Ryde St John's Road with a Ryde-Ventnor train leaving behind O2 Class 0-4-4T No W23 *Totland*, on Saturday 17 April 1948. St John's Road was the original terminus at Ryde for both the Newport and Ventnor lines; it was also the site of an important locomotive works.
*Pursey Short*

Another photograph of the early nationalisation days, this time at Sandown, on 30 May 1948. O2 Class No W33 *Bembridge* stands at the platform with an evening Ryde Pier Head to Ventnor train. Sandown was also the junction for the Merstone and Newport line, and, of course, was one of the Island's premier holiday destinations.
*Pursey Short*

A Summer Sunday Ventnor-Newport train leaves Sandown on the evening of 1 July 1951 behind O2 No W25 *Godshill*. Opened in stages 1875/79, the line closed in February 1956. *Pursey Short*

sheet on access to the Island by three alternative routes from Waterloo, namely the Portsmouth Direct route to Ryde; to Southampton for Cowes; and to Lymington for Freshwater, Yarmouth and the 'Western Wight'. That same timetable also included details and illustrative advertisements for the car ferry from Lymington. The regular Island services for all three companies were also included.

Once in control, the Southern Railway made valuable improvements to the Island's railways and to the means of access via the ferry service. Ryde Pier provided the introduction to the Island with all the vital first impressions. Rebuilding, begun by the Southern Railway, was completed for July 1933. The first stage involving the renewal of the first half of the pier was completed in June 1925. The second section, the seaward end of the pier and the Pier Head station, was then undertaken. Again, reinforced concrete piles with bracings, beams and decking were steadily set into the sea and work was also commenced on the station. The latter, described as 'obsolete buildings in need of demolition', was replaced by much improved and enlarged accommodation offering four platforms. Ryde St Johns Road was also rebuilt and 'new' signal boxes were provided at St Johns Road, this structure formerly doing service at Waterloo *SECR*, and at Smallbrook Junction. Until 1926 these two lines were independent of each other, relating back to the old companies practice, but in that year a cross-over was installed to allow for double-line working to and from Ryde Pier Head during the busy season.

As the line carrying the heaviest summer traffic, the Ryde-Ventnor section saw several useful improvements. A crossing loop was installed at Wroxhall, between Shanklin and Ventnor, being opened in Summer 1924,

and the entire section between Brading and Sandown was doubled in 1927 making services to and from Ventnor considerably easier to operate. Included in its programme of new works, presented in January 1927, the Southern Railway costed the project at £28,000. Reconstruction of Newport station, £25,500, and further work at Smallbrook and Haven Street were also included. On the Ryde-Newport line a passing place was provided at Haven Street. Here, the original station consisting of one platform with simple timber accommodation was removed to provide a new masonry structure separate from the new island platform, on the north side of the line. The work was completed in June 1926. Whippingham, between Wootton and Newport, was also a passing place, the original station site here being built for Queen Victoria as access to Osborne House. The passing loop at Ashey station between Smallbrook Junction and Haven Street, an original placement, was removed with the provision of the new crossing at Haven Street. Further west, on the Freshwater line, there were also examples of excess crossing places being removed as at Carisbrooke and Yarmouth, also at Whitwell, the latter being on the Newport-Ventnor West line. Freshwater station, however, was upgraded in 1927 when the platform and station buildings were extended, the layout altered, and a new signal box installed. Such improvements undoubtedly reflected the growth in traffic and the fact that Freshwater was the terminus for Totland Bay, Alum Bay, The Needles and, of course, Freshwater Bay itself. An interesting development in services involving Freshwater, came in July 1933 when a through Ventnor-Freshwater working was introduced. It was a definite boon to tourism exploiting the potential of the railway system. The morning departure from

Ventnor was at 9.55 am arriving Freshwater at 11.16 am. The return departed at 5.20 pm arriving Ventnor at 6.48 pm.

One of the Southern Railway's most essential tasks was the replacement of locomotives and rolling stock. Given the steady increase in tourist traffic to the Island new provision was imperative. With regard to locomotion the major effect was felt with the eventual transfer to the Island of twenty-three 02 0-4-4T ex London and South Western stock. These arrived from 1923 to as late as 1949, numbers 19 'Osborne' and 20 'Shanklin' being the first, in May 1923, whilst numbers 35 'Freshwater' and 36 'Carisbrooke' arrived in 1949. Four E1 0-6-0T of London Brighton and South Coast origin, numbered 1-4, and named 'Medina', 'Yarmouth', 'Ryde' and 'Wroxhall', together with three A1X 0-6-0T numbered 9 'Fishbourne', 13 'Carisbrooke' and 14 'Bembridge' arrived between June 1927 and July 1932. The 'Terrier' A1X locomotives were subsequently returned to the mainland – 'Fishbourne' and 'Bembridge' in 1936 and 'Carisbrooke' in 1949. Heavier locomotives, such as the 02 class, required that lines be strengthened where necessary, particularly in the case of bridges on the Freshwater route from Newport. The locomotive turntable at Bembridge was another structure requiring rebuilding to allow for the larger 02 class locos to work the branch. Rebuilding took place in 1936. Rebuilding at Ryde St Johns locomotive depot had been completed, earlier, in May 1930.

Increased tourist traffic also required adequate rolling stock to meet the demand. As with motive power, the Southern introduced main line stock from the London Chatham and Dover Railway together with sets from the London Brighton and South Coast, South Eastern and Chatham and London South Western Railways.

Traffic levels, as the following comparative details will show, demanded that the Island keep pace with tourist demand. During the Summer of 1914, for example, there were 17 trains in each direction serving Ryde and Ventnor, this being the fullest Saturday service. By 1931 there were 36 trains each way on Saturdays. Likewise, between Ryde and Newport there were 11 trains in 1914 and 16 in 1931. Looking at Sunday service for these two particular years, there were 7 trains in each direction between Ryde and Ventnor in the Summer of 1914 and 18 in 1931. The figures for Sunday service are particularly useful in any study of tourism as they are a definite pointer to shifting leisure habits reflecting much greater mobility and the desire to use free time to the full.

Since 1880 the steamers on the Portsmouth-Ryde service were owned and operated jointly by *LBSCR* and *LSWR*. From 1923 the Southern also introduced new paddle steamers to gradually replace older craft. Between 1889 and 1911 five ships worked between Portsmouth and Ryde, but in 1924 the Southern introduced a new paddle steamer, 'Shanklin'. This was followed by 'Merstone' and 'Portsdown' in 1928 and 'Southsea' and 'Whippingham' in 1930. Two further orders were placed for 'Sandown', 1934, and 'Ryde', 1937. The *Southern Railway Magazine* for January 1934 gave details for its then newest vessel on order:

The Company have placed an order with Messrs Wm Denny and Bros., of Dumbarton for a paddle steamer for the Portsmouth-Ryde service.

The dimensions of the new paddle steamer will be: length, 233 ft; breadth, 29 ft; draft, 6ft 9 in.

A fine shot of 02 No W15 *Cowes* with its 'British Railways' logo, standing outside the 'new' works building of 1930 vintage at St. John's. 9 October 1948
*Pursey Short*

Two generations of Isle of Wight ferries both seen at Portsmouth Harbour. The Southern Railway's paddle steamer *Sandown* is seen at the railway jetty on Sunday 20 May 1948. The ship was built for the Company in 1934. The newer, post-war image is represented in this view of the Motor Vessel *Southsea* seen at the Harbour in May 1949. Note also the Gosport ferries active around the new ship. *Southsea* entered service in 1948 together with sister vessel, *Brading*; *Shanklin* followed in 1951. *Pursey Short*

The Isle of Wight Railway opened from Shanklin to Ventnor on 10 September 1866, two years after the Ryde-Shanklin section. A heavy climb inland through Wroxall took the line up to St Boniface Down from where it descended to Ventnor through St Boniface Down Tunnel 1,312 yards long. Ventnor station occupied an extensive quarried cutting, 276 feet above the sea, and in this view, taken on 27 July 1935, 02 No.W22 *Brading* leaves the tunnel and enters the terminus. The open wagons show their S.R. parentage.

*S.W. Baker*

Sandown and the famous landmark of sorts, the elevated signal box which remained in use until as late as 1989. In this view 02 No. W33, *Bembridge*, displays its Southern identity at the platform in June. 1937.
*S.W. Baker*

Another rural branch, from Brading to Bembridge, served the latter's coastal community which during the later nineteenth century encouraged steamer traffic from the mainland. The Bembridge branch, $2^3/4$ miles, opened in May 1882, closing in 1953. In this view, O2 No 15 *Cowes* is seen leaving the terminus for Brading on 1 July 1951.
*Pursey Short*

the vessel will have a speed of 14½ knots and she will be licensed to carry about 900 passengers. She will have triple expansion engines and will be ready to take her place on the service in July next.

The Southern's magazine went on, in the same article, to record the evidence of increased traffic, drawing comparisons with the past to illustrate the progress made:

These new boats mark a very big improvement in the transport facilities to the Island, and that this is appreciated by the travelling public is evidenced by the remarkable growth in numbers of passengers carried on this route. In 1913 the number conveyed was 845,000 whilst in 1930 this had grown to 2,212,994. The peak of traffic is reached during August and on the Saturday following the August Week-End last year (1933), 46,659 passengers were conveyed, a record total for any one day.

Ironically, the Southern Railway's initiative in terms of 'Drive On, Drive Off' ferry services from Portsmouth to Fishbourne and Lymington to Yarmouth was a definite factor in the long-term competition from road transport on the Isle of Wight. 'Southern Vectis' bus services from the thirties onward made themselves significant competitors. Some measure of the number of private cars can be seen in the fact that in 1937 the Portsmouth-Fishbourne service carried 24,000 cars; the Lymington-Yarmouth crossing carried 1,700. On 1 May 1938, however, the Southern Railway introduced its new 'Drive On' facility at Lymington Quay. Equipped to carry 16-20 cars and 400 passengers, the new ship 'Lymington' represented a whole new experience, far removed from the antiquated practice of towing barges, which had been the only method available before 1938 at Lymington. The *Southern Railway Magazine*, described its new ship in amusing imagery: "She can travel sideways like a crab and waltzes around in small circles". It was also pointed out that cars on the Lymington-Yarmouth crossing numbered 297 for Easter 1939, as against only 65 the previous year. Not the best news for rail services, overall. A later addition, 'Farringford' entered service n 1947, but at Portsmouth with its far more intensive facilities, three ships were at work by 1930 – 'Fishbourne', beginning in 1927, 'Wootton' 1928, and 'Hilsea' in 1930.

An appropriate reference with which to end this basic survey would be to holiday traffic, in this case, to Shanklin, as recorded in the *Southern Railway Magazine* for September 1939. Reporting on that August Bank Holiday weekend, which in many ways marked the end of an era, we read:

Shanklin was again well to the fore with a total of 14,360 Monthly tickets collected on the Saturday alone, representing an increase of 6,800 over the same day last year. The number of Monthly tickets collected in the Island for the Saturday was no less than 32,300 together with 1,500 Week End tickets. This is apart from day excursions and normal traffic.

A number of visitors arrived on the Island without first making sure of their accommodation, and in consequence most towns reported 'sleeping in the open' for one or more nights.

Just over two years later, in the early morning of 20 September 1941, the paddle steamer 'Portsdown' struck a mine whilst working to Ryde. My father often spoke of it, telling me how it woke the city of Portsmouth. It was another world, far removed from that of tourism.

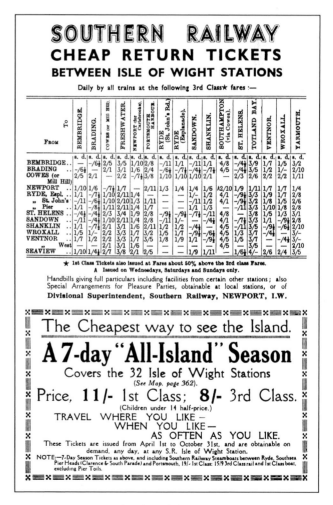

*Hints for Holidays, 1939*

# MOTORING IN THE ISLE OF WIGHT.

Loading Motor Cars at Lymington.

NO Motor Tour through England can be considered complete which does not include a run round the Isle of Wight (sixty miles). The most convenient point for crossing is at Lymington, on the South side of the charming New Forest, where the London and South Western Railway Company has provided efficient accommodation for such traffic, including slipways whereby cars can be shipped by their own power, on to specially constructed boats, thus entirely obviating the necessity of lifting, and removing a difficulty which hitherto has deterred many from visiting the lovely "Garden Isle."

The boats—towed by fast, powerful tugs—quickly negotiate the passage, which is the shortest and most sheltered, to the island. On Week-days (weather and circumstances permitting) the boats leave Lymington Town Station Wharf at 9*30, 11.30 a.m., 2.30 and 4.45 p.m. for Yarmouth, and leave Yarmouth at 8.*0 a.m., 12.30, 3.15 and 5.30 p.m. for Lymington. Cars should be upon the Wharf half-an-hour before these times.

\* Prior notice should be given to the Station Master at Lymington in regard to conveyance by these boats.

**Special passages can be arranged on Sundays upon arrangement being made with the Station Master, Lymington (Telephone No. 7), not later than the previous day, the extra charge being £1 per Car above the ordinary rates, which are 9s. for cars not exceeding half-a-ton, and 14s. for cars above 10 cwts., including wharfage and porterage at Lymington and Yarmouth.**

## BANK HOLIDAYS ARE TREATED AS ORDINARY WEEK-DAYS; GOOD FRIDAY AND CHRISTMAS DAY AS SUNDAYS.

Unloading Motor Cars at Yarmouth, I. of W.

Newport was the commercial, administrative capital and a very important railway centre on the Island. All parts of the railway system were easily accessible from Newport. In this view from April 1948 O2 No 28 *Ashey* leaves Newport for Ryde.     *Pursey Short*

Newport also gave access to Freshwater and Yarmouth as the following three pictures illustrate. In the first, a Sunday Newport-Freshwater train is seen leaving Newport with O2 No. 29 *Alverstone* in charge. 16 April 1950.     *Pursey Short*

## Chapter Three
# EXPANSION AND ENTERPRISE

The railway layout at Northam, relating to the siting of the South Western's original terminus at Southampton, gave a clear indication that, initially, there were no immediate plans for extensions westward. As a result of this, later expansion and the heavy traffic this century suffered the operational hindrance of the severe Northam curve, leading around westward, avoiding the terminus, towards what became Southampton Central. When rails were laid westward to Weymouth, this route was less than direct, being a single line serving as many centres of population, trade and industry as possible – Brockenhurst, Ringwood, Wimborne and Wareham, all of them junction stations at some stage. The Southampton and Dorchester opened on 1 June 1847; Bournemouth, such as it was at that time, was not a factor and played no part in the considerations, social, economic or otherwise.

For the first ten years of its existence the line offered the only through rail link between London and the communities of West Hampshire and Dorset, and with the increase in traffic and trade the line was doubled from Redbridge to Wimborne between August 1857 and

September 1858 and westward to Dorchester for 1 August 1863. Further eastward, the Northam triangle was installed in August 1858 removing the need for reversal at Southampton Terminus. Shortly before this, however, on 20 January 1857, the Great Western Railway opened its line southward from Yeovil to Weymouth with its direct service from the Dorset coast to Paddington. *LSWR* trains had access from Dorchester to Weymouth, the seven mile section being laid in for the mixed gauge working. Great Western services had nominal rights to work eastward from Dorchester over the *LSWR* as far as Moreton, where the mixed gauge ended.

To celebrate the arrival of the railway at Weymouth the *Southern Times* wrote of the dawning of the 'Golden Age': 'The railway is open and our town now enters really into the bustle of trade'. It continued in its congratulatory mood by focussing on the element of choice now open to the people of both Weymouth and Dorchester when travelling to London – "The Great Western, or broad gauge with a distance of $168\frac{1}{2}$ miles or the South Western, on the narrow gauge, distance $147\frac{1}{4}$ miles".

### GREAT WESTERN RAILWAY.
#### Up Trains.

| DAILY. | 1 & 2 CLASS. | 1, 2, 3 CLASS. | 1 & 2 CLASS. | 1 & 2 CLASS. | 1 & 2 CLASS. | 1 & 2 CLASS. |
|---|---|---|---|---|---|---|
| | a.m. | a.m. | a.m. | p.m. | p.m. | p.m. |
| FROM Weymouth | 6.15 | 8.30 | 10.30 | 12.30 | 4.10 | 6.0 |
| Dorchester | 6.30 | 8.50 | 10.50 | 12.50 | 4.30 | 6.20 |
| Yeovil | 7.10 | 9.45 | 11.45 | 1.35 | 5.15 | 7.10 |
| Westbury | 8.10 | 10.55 | 12.48 | 2.40 | 6.15 | 8.18 |
| Chippenham | 8.53 | 11.40 | 1.30 | 3.25 | 7.0 | — |
| London | 11.25 | 7.30 | 4.46 | 6.0 | 10.35 | |

#### Down Trains.

| DAILY. | 1, 2, 3 CLASS. | 1 & 2 CLASS.* | 1 & 2 CLASS. | 1 & 2 CLASS. | 1 & 2 CLASS. | 1 & 2 CLASS. |
|---|---|---|---|---|---|---|
| | a.m. | a.m. | a.m. | a.m. | p.m. | p.m. |
| FROM London | — | 6.0 | 9.40 | 11.0 | 12.50 | 4.50 |
| Chippenham | — | 9.45 | 12.10 | 2.0 | 4.30 | 7.0 |
| Westbury | — | 10.30 | 12.50 | 2.40 | 5.10 | 7.57 |
| Yeovil | 9.0 | 11.45 | 2.0 | 3.45 | 6.30 | 9.0 |
| Dorchester | 9.55 | 12.45 | 2.45 | 4.30 | 7.20 | 9.45 |
| Weymouth | 10.15 | 1.5 | 3.5 | 4.50 | 7.40 | 10.5 |

* Third-class from London, Didcot, and Reading to Frome and intermediate stations to Weymouth.

### LONDON AND SOUTH-WESTERN RAILWAY.
#### Up Trains.

| DAILY. | 1 & 2 CLASS. | 1, 2, 3 CLASS. | 1 & 2 CLASS. | 1 & 2 CLASS. | 1 & 2 CLASS. | 1, 2, 3 CLASS. | 1 & 2 MAIL. | |
|---|---|---|---|---|---|---|---|---|
| | a.m. | a.m. | a.m. | p.m. | p.m. | p.m. | p.m. | |
| FROM Weymouth | 6.0 | 8.0 | 11.55 | 12.45 | 4.15 | 5.45 | 9.45 | — |
| Dorchester | 6.25 | 8.25 | 12.20 | 1.15 G | 4.40 | 6.30 G | 10.15 | |
| Southampton | 8.50 | 12.30 | 3.0 | 6.20 arr. | 7.10 | 10.40 arr. | 1.30 | — |
| Waterloo | 11.5 | 5.0 | 5.55 | 9.20 | 9.55 | — | 4.30 | — |

G. These are goods trains from Dorchester to Southampton, to which passenger carriages are attached.

#### Down Trains.

| DAILY. | 1 & 2 CLASS. | 1, 2, 3 CLASS. | 1 & 2 CLASS. | 1 & 2 CLASS. | Exp. G. | 1ST CLASS EXP. | 1 & 2 CLASS. | 1 & 2 MAIL. |
|---|---|---|---|---|---|---|---|---|
| | | a.m. | a.m. | a.m. | a.m. | | | |
| FROM Waterloo | A | 6.0 | 9.40 | 10.15 | 11.0 | 3.0 | 5.0 | 8.30 |
| Southampton | 6.30 | 10.30 | — | 1.30 | — | 5.40 | 7.45 | 12.6 |
| Dorchester | 11.40 | 1.20 | — | 4.0 | — | 8.5 | 10.10 | 3.0 |
| Weymouth | 12.0 | 1.40 | — | 4.20 | — | 8.25 | 10.30 | — |

A. Goods train from Southampton to Dorchester, to which passenger carriages are attached.
G. This train conveys first-class passengers only, with the exception of servants in actual attendance upon their employers.

*Opposite top:* The same locomotive No 29, is seen again here, this time entering Yarmouth station on 10 September 1953. Note the signboard for the ferry service to Lymington.
*R.C. Riley*

*Opposite bottom:* At Freshwater terminus – for Totland Bay and Alum Bay – O2 No 33 *Bembridge* runs around its train having worked in the 12.40 pm service from Newport. The Newport, Yarmouth and Freshwater Railway opened in July 1889 and was an inevitable victim of early closure in September 1953.
*R.C. Riley*

*The Royal Wessex* complete with its new Mark One standard coaching stock – the *Festival of Britain* train – is seen here having passed St Denys, heading into Southampton.  Light Pacific, 'West Country' Class 4-6-2 No 34107 *Blandford Forum* is in charge, Saturday 14 July 1951.
*Pursey Short*

An illustration of the restriction to the main line posed by Northam Curve.  *The Bournemouth Belle* headed by 'Merchant Navy' Pacific, No 35014, *Nederland Line* passes under Northam bridge.  11 June 1949.

*Pursey Short*

Leaving Southampton Central on a Salisbury-Portsmouth working in June 1952. The coaching stock is ex GWR; the locomotive, an N Class 2-6-0, No 31852.

At the opposite, west end of the station, 'Merchant Navy' No 35010 *Blue Star* leaves Southampton Central with a Waterloo-Bournemouth working, 13 May 1953. Note the famous signal gantry and characteristic flat-roof signal box.
*R.C. Riley*

Dorchester (South) the western terminus of the original Southampton and Dorchester Railway of 1847. The 'up' side buildings reflect that of a terminus whilst also representing the hopes of expansion westward on a coastal route to Exeter which was never to be. The 'down' platform follows the curve around to join with the ex GWR/Wilts and Weymouth line into Weymouth itself, opened in 1857.
In this view, looking westward, 'King Arthur', No 30739, *King Leodegrance*, has just reversed into the 'up' platform, off the main line. The train is the 2.20 pm Weymouth-Andover Junction, formed of ex LSWR non corridor stock. 27 August 1954.
*R.C.Riley*

36

It was all very different at Bournemouth. With a population of 1707, in 1861, the year that saw the opening of the resort's first wooden pier, 1000 feet long, Bournemouth was woefully distant from the vital railway links that would guarantee its growth. There was growth, however, as population figures for 1871 reflected an increase to 5,896 and again, a significant rise to 16,859 for 1881. Useful evidence as to the intention and achievement of the local authority is found in the records of the Local Government Board. The Eighth Annual Report, 1878/79, reveals that at that time, Bournemouth secured the following finances: £22,833 to construct a new pier, £9,000 for sewerage works, £1,075 for purpose of paving and drainage together with £500 for a steam roller! Progressive development was the keynote; the Lord Mayor of London opened the new pier in 1880. An enterprising local authority, determined to develop the resort, was somewhat at odds with the London South Western Railway and its seemingly elliptical response towards communications with Bournemouth but there were developments, not least, the emergence of the Somerset and Dorset line from Bath and the threat of invasion by the Great Western.

Taking events in order, the first improvement for Bournemouth offering anything other than the alternative of the short ferry crossing from Hamworthy and road from Poole eastward, or the road journey of some eight miles south-westward from Christchurch Road (Holmsley) on the Southampton and Dorchester line, was the opening of the single line from Ringwood to Christchurch. Following the River Avon, via Hurn, the Ringwood, Christchurch and Bournemouth opened on 13 November 1862. An extension to Bournemouth itself was opened on 14 March 1870.

Ringwood, as the largest centre of population, and the junction for Bournemouth East from March 1870, was the most important intermediate station on the original *LSWR* route into Dorset. The main buildings were on the 'up' side and a covered footbridge linked the two platforms – the 'up' 339 feet, and the 'down' which also served the loop for the Bournemouth line, 405 feet. From Ringwood, the main line westward and the branch ran side by side, first crossing the River Avon, whereafter the branch curved southward following close by the west bank of the river to Christchurch. A mile or so south of the junction at Ringwood, the line wound its way past Avon Lodge Halt, the private property of Lord Egmont, Avon Castle being on the banks of the river between Avon and the railway. It opened on 3 November 1862 and closed along with the entire line on 20 September 1935.

Bournemouth got its East station with the extension from Christchurch in 1870; it got its 'West' station in June 1874. The Poole and Bournemouth Railway was authorised in the mid 1860s to link both these towns with the South Western main line at Broadstone. Being subject to modified arrangements, what eventually transpired was the opening of this important link in two stages: Broadstone to Poole on 2 December 1872, and Poole to Bournemouth West on 15 June 1874.

Without doubt, the completion and opening of the Somerset and Dorset Railway's Bath extension from Evercreech Junction over the Mendips to Bath offered tremendous potential for Bournemouth as a resort. The new line, orientated towards the Midlands and the North, opened on 20 July 1874. With reversal at Wimborne, Somerset and Dorset trains could now run into Bournemouth West. At the northern end, the Midland Railway route from Mangotsfield to Bath opened on 7 May 1870; from Mangotsfield northward the Midland Railway to Birmingham comprised the Birmingham and Gloucester opening on December 17 1840 and the Bristol and Gloucester Railway opened on 6 July 1844. The service was further improved just over ten years later when, under an Act of 20 August 1883, a cut-off was provided from Corfe Mullen (S & D) south-westward directly onto the South Western main line at Broadstone. Passenger services to Bath and beyond began over the cut-off on 1 November 1886.

Although the Somerset and Dorset main line became famous for its long-distance summer traffic it was an extremely difficult line to work on an intensive basis with such traffic. Severe gradients, and many of them, the winding nature of the line, and the fact that there were 23 miles of single line, presented problems. On both sides of Masbury Summit, for example, there were long sections of 1 in 50 working. Coming south, this was much the case between Radstock and the summit, with a distance of some seven miles unbroken climb, whilst northbound trains faced a slightly longer but equally steep climb from Evercreech. Double-heading was inevitable. The single line sections, working southward, were: Bath Junction – Midford 3 miles 68 chains, Templecombe No 2 Jnct – Blandford the longest section at 16 miles 27 chains and Corfe Mullen – Broadstone 3 miles. During the summer of 1914, for example, the fastest service between Bath and Bournemouth was 1 hour 54 minutes.

As at Ringwood, serving a reasonable centre of population and acting as a junction for Bournemouth East, so it was at Wimborne. Not only an ancient Minster, Wimborne was also a relative centre of population, market trade and agriculture within the larger area; it was also the junction for the Somerset and Dorset from the summer of 1874. Another junction station on the original Southampton and Dorchester main line was that of West Moors, five miles east. It was the junction for the Salisbury and Dorset Junction Railway opening on 20 December 1866. The line offered useful access from Bournemouth and the Dorset coastal area to Bristol, South Wales, the West of England, and the Midlands via Salisbury.

The final junction station for purposes of this survey of the South Western's original main line (there was another further west at Wareham for Swanage) was Broadstone. Once the Corfe Mullen curve of 1885 had removed the need for the Somerset and Dorset trains to run into Wimborne and reverse onto *LSWR* tracks, Broadstone assumed much greater significance. The Somerset and Dorset trains came off their single line route to cross the Southampton and Dorchester line to gain the Bournemouth route. There were three platforms at Broadstone, each one 640 feet in length, the main buildings being on the 'down' Bournemouth side. The island platforms served the 'up' Bournemouth-Ringwood service and the Somerset Dorset line and, on the opposite face, the 'down' Weymouth line. The far platform was for the 'up' Weymouth-Southampton services.

The Solent area and surrounding district was definitive *LSWR* territory so much so that concerned interests in Bournemouth, impatient with the company's apparent lack of initiative, questioned its monopoly. Overtures were made in the early eighties to

The midday Bournemouth West, Ringwood and Brockenhurst service calls at Poole on 6 August 1962 with M7 No 30105 up front. From the appearance of the open platform it seems that there was the inevitable Bank Holiday weather that day!
*M. Mensing*

Creekmoor Halt between Poole and Broadstone was opened on 19 January 1933 as a reflection of the growing residential character of that area. In August 1962 the 3.40 pm Bournemouth West-Bristol stopping service over the S & D via Bath, was headed by Class 9F 2-10-0 No 92245, something of a humiliating task for such a powerful, capable locomotive. Creekmoor closed on 17 March 1966.
*M. Mensing*

Parkstone, between Bournemouth and Poole, shows evidence of its LSWR heritage in this view on August Bank Holiday 6 August 1962. 2-6-0 'U' Class No 31795 arrives at the station with the 12.50 Salisbury-Bournemouth West via the Fordingbridge, West Moors and Wimborne route. *M. Mensing*

Yet another route through to Parkstone was the push/pull service from Brockenhurst via the original main line through Ringwood to Bournemouth West. 0-4-4T M7 No 30105 is in charge here – propelling its train into Parkstone – the 2.03 pm Brockenhurst-Bournemouth West. 6 August 1962. *M. Mensing*

Precedent and prestige at Bournemouth Central! Here, a Gresley Class V2 2-6-2 on loan from the Eastern Region leaves with the 'up' *Bournemouth Belle* resplendent with its Pullman stock. The Bulleid Pacifics were temporarily withdrawn for axle testing at this time early/mid 1953 after No 35030 *Bibby Line* suffered a fractured driving axle whilst in traffic at Crewkerne. 30 April 1953.

*R.C. Riley*

Bournemouth's main locomotive depot close to Central station presented something of an image problem in such a well regarded residential area but despite the warnings about excessive noise and nuisance, the work of this busy shed had to progress. In this view 'King Arthur' No 30753 *Melisande* is on the turntable with its 'British Railways' logo whilst, beyond, 'Merchant Navy', No 21C11 later numbered 35011, *General Steam Navigation* takes water.

*Pursey Short*

the Great Western Railway who planned to enter the area via the Didcot, Newbury and Southampton Railway, whereby *GWR* interests reached Winchester so as to break the South Western's monopoly. It was the reverse of the situation at Plymouth and in Cornwall during the previous decade when, weary of the Great Western's seeming lack of initiative, local interests actively courted the *LSWR*. Fear of any possible incursion by the Great Western, the growing stature of Bournemouth as a resort and the appointment of Charles Scotter, an extremely able and energetic General Manager, keen for innovations, brought about the necessary action – the 'direct' route westward into Bournemouth from Brockenhurst.

From 5 March 1888 Bournemouth benefited from its new direct access, also its new station, Bournemouth Central, and the rail link with Bournemouth West. The work was completed in stages. Authorised on 20 August 1883, the largest and most important of a number of related works inaugurated on that date, the Bournemouth 'direct' line involved construction of 10½ miles of railway from Lymington Junction, east of Brockenhurst to Christchurch, where the new line met the existing route, via Ringwood.

An important feature of the works was the New Bournemouth East station (renamed 'Central' on 1 May 1899) opened on 20 July 1885. Ornate metalwork supported a magnificent overall glazed roof with distinguished glazed panelled windscreens at each end blended with the reddish-brown brickwork of the main walls. The extensive sweep of the building was enhanced by regular pilasters with lancet windows grouped in threes. A subway provided access between platforms, whilst strict segregation was practised in class terms for waiting rooms, even toilets, with third class separated. Two further developments followed in 1886; the opening

of a new station for Christchurch on 30 May 1886, together with the introduction of double-track working between these new stations of Christchurch and Bournemouth. Another new station, that at Boscombe, was also opened on 1 July 1886. (The island platform here was later (1932) reopened as a quadrupled layout giving two inner through lines and outer platforms ('up' and 'down').

Following the developments of the early and mid summer of 1886, and the new Bournemouth station of the previous year, it took until the Spring of 1888 to complete the programme. On 5 March 1888 the 'direct' route from Brockenhurst to Christchurch was opened. The link line between Bournemouth East and West was also opened that day, Bournemouth East becoming the through station, it remains today.

At the eastern end of the new line, Brockenhurst was rebuilt. It was a busy station, as the junction for Lymington and as a centre for New Forest excursions. The main buildings were on the 'up' side – this was an island platform with a loop. The 'down' side also had a bay platform. Redevelopment in 1936 saw the conversion of the 'down' bay into a loop line. Extended canopies, a feature of this period for all the four companies at important stations together with modern lighting etc. kept Brockenhurst up to image. Between Brockenhurst and Christchurch the new stations provided were: Sway, New Milton (Milton until May 1897), Hinton Admiral (Hinton until May 1888). Further west, Boscombe became Pokestone from October 1891 and a new Boscombe station was brought into use on 1 June 1897. The latter was better sited to serve the community and was situated immediately south of King's Park, itself adjoining Little Down Common and nearby Queen' Park, all useful locations in promoting positive images of the community.

Into Hampshire's magnificent New Forest landscape. Here, rebuilt 'West Country' 4-6-2, No 34040 *Crewkerne* heads a train of mixed Southern and B.R. standard stock making up the 10.30 am Waterloo-Bournemouth. 10 September 1966.

*M. Mensing*

Lymington Junction on 10 September 1966. Birmingham RCW/Sulzer, 1550 H.P. later classified Class 33, D6501 takes the LMS stock of the 10.30 am Poole-York past the junction, west of the station – a time of considerable change; note the conductor rails in place.
*M. Mensing*

On the Lymington branch – M7 0-4-4T No 30111 stands at the distinctive Lymington Town station with a Lymington Pier – Brockenhurst train on Sunday 15 July, 1951.
*Pursey Short*

A Standard Class 4 No 75075 on a Bournemouth-bound working is seen here approaching Sway on 10 September 1966. Steam has less than a year's life to go and yet were it not for the presence of the 'third rail', there is little enough evidence from the photograph to reflect any other significant change e.g. the familiar upper quadrant distant signal.                                          *M. Mensing*

The English summer, New Milton and the New Forest environment. This is very much a portrait of what many people took to embody the stability and permanence of the railway and, indeed, life generally during the fifties. 'King Arthur' Class 4-6-0 No 30765 *Sir Gareth* is seen here on an 'up' stopping train of mixed stock. It was the 28 June 1957 and one can almost feel the sunshine and experience the shadows and shade given off here.                                          *R.C. Riley*

Moving back into Bournemouth itself we see another 'King Arthur' Class, this time No 30743 *Lyonesse* posing light engine at Central station. Note the distinctive lines of the locomotive as seen from this angle set off no less by the equally imposing quality and proportions of the station architecture itself. 24 July 1954.

R.C.Riley

Southern Railway publicity did its duty towards Bournemouth as the accompanying chapter shows. *Hints for Holidays* was a principal showcase in this respect, so, too, were those prestigious train services, the 'named' workings, that caught the imagination, enhancing the imagery and association of both the Southern Railway, and Bournemouth as a distinguished national resort. Reputation was everything.

The famous 'named' trains serving Bournemouth between the Wars were – *The Pines Express*, *The Bournemouth Limited* and *The Bournemouth Belle*.

*The Pines Express* did not actually receive its title until 1927 but the service dated back to October 1910. It was the most prestigious of the many services from Manchester and its surrounding district to the South Coast area between Portsmouth and Poole. *The Pines* was also the most distinguished service over the Somerset and Dorset line. Coming south from Manchester London Road over the ex *LNWR* to Birmingham, it then followed the ex Midland route south to Mangotsfield, thence to Bath and the Somerset and Dorset Joint Line, to the LSWR at Broadstone, and, finally, Bournemouth West.

*The Bournemouth Limited*, a notable express service from Waterloo, was introduced on 8 July 1929 but had earlier been running as an unnamed timetabled working dating from the turn of the century. *The Limited* was a 2 hour, non-stop service to and from Bournemouth Central departing there at 8.40 am with the return departure from Waterloo at 4.30pm. The two hour non-stop service was firmly established by 1914, the Summer timetable for that year showing a 9.08 am departure from Bournemouth Central with a return working departing Waterloo at 4.10 pm. In the absence of water troughs this was a significant achievement, helped, not least, by Joseph Locke's magnificent route south-westward and the progressive improvements to the main line thereafter. Together with the introduction of the *Bournemouth Limited*, the Southern also upgraded its services northward, in particular, its Bournemouth West – Manchester and Birkenhead, and its through service to Newcastle.

# WATERLOO-BOURNEMOUTH IN 2 HOURS.

## The "Bournemouth Limited."

*The 2-hour non-stop Corridor and Restaurant Car Express which runs on weekdays between Bournemouth and Waterloo.*

| | |
|---|---|
| Bournemouth dep. 8.40 a.m. | Waterloo . dep. 4.30 p.m. |
| Waterloo . arr. 10.40 „ | Bournemouth arr. 6.30 „ |

Seats Booked 1/- (*See Page* 14).

Bournemouth West on Saturday 21 July 1951 sees 'Britannia' Pacific 4-6-2 No 70009 *Alfred The Great* leaving with *The Bournemouth Belle*. The train is receiving assistance from an 0-4-4T M7 'banker'. Bournemouth West was the terminus for all the holiday traffic routed over the S & D line and was served by its own shed facilities at nearby Branksome.

*Pursey Short*

Of all the services between Waterloo and Bournemouth, *The Bournemouth Belle* was the most exclusive, prestigious working. Pullman coaches had made their appearance on Bournemouth services in 1890, but *The Bournemouth Belle* was the first all-Pullman formation. Introduced on 5 July 1931, the new train was promoted by the Southern Railway so as to:

.... rank with other famous Pullman expresses such as the *Southern Belle, Queen of Scots* and *Golden Arrow* ...

The *Southern Railway Magazine* celebrated its distinguished new service:

On Sunday 5 July, the Southern Railway in conjunction with the Pullman Car Company, inaugurated an all-Pullman service between London and Bournemouth. The new train which is called *The Bournemouth Belle* leaves London at 10.30 am every day and returns from Bournemouth at 4.50 pm.

The approximate weight of the train without locomotive is 384 tons (10 cars A-K, three first class E-G) and it has a total seating capacity of 74 first class and 240 third class. Four of the cars are equipped with kitchens...

The exteriors of all the cars are painted in Pullman standard colours, viz, umber and cream relieved with gold lines ....

In accordance with the usual Pullman practice, the interior decoration of each car varies, and some particularly pleasant results have been achieved. A feature of the *Bournemouth Belle* is the introduction for the first time of an improved type of third-class Pullman car. Four new third-class cars have been built by the Birmingham Railway Carriage and Wagon Co Ltd. The new third-class saloons are panelled throughout in mahogany inlaid in modern style in colours of blue. The floor covering is of rubber in a tiled design, either in two shades of green and black or in two shades of blue and black. The seating is upholstered either in a camel ground of floral moquette or a moquette with dark green of trellis design. The brass furniture is finished in gilt and the floor covering in the vestibule and corridors is of a rubber tiling in green and white.

The train departed from Waterloo at 10.30 am on weekdays and Sundays, arriving at Bournemouth Central at 12.39 pm with one stop at Southampton (11.59 am). On weekdays there was also a portion of the train for Dorchester and Weymouth, (cars F-H) arriving at the latter at 1.45 pm and departing at 4 pm. The 'up' working from Bournemouth Central, weekdays and Sundays, departed at 5.10 pm arriving Southampton at 5.50 pm and Waterloo at 7.18 pm.

In its initial promotional work for *The Bournemouth Belle*, the *Southern Railway Magazine* recorded that 'a number of guests and Press representatives' were invited on the inaugural run. On arrival at Bournemouth the party was received by the Deputy Mayor on behalf of the Corporation, who took them for a tour of Bournemouth and entertained them to afternoon tea at the new Pavilion. This had also been the case with *The Limited*.

By 1939 the 'down' departure from Waterloo was set at 10.30 am for both weekdays and Sundays, arriving Southampton at 11.57 am and Bournemouth Central 12.36 pm, Bournemouth West, 12.47 pm. In the 'up' direction departure from Bournemouth West was 4.35 pm, Central 4.45 pm, Southampton depart 5.20 pm and Waterloo arriving 6.45 pm. The 'up' train on Sundays had the different departure time of 6.30 pm, Bournemouth West, 6.40 pm, Central, 7.20 pm Southampton and arrival at Waterloo at 8.45 pm.

High standards in timing and performance over the main line westward from Waterloo to Southampton and Bournemouth owed much to the expertise of the civil engineers – to Locke's original efforts in the late 1830s, and again, to the quadrupling of the main line to Basingstoke and Worting Junction. Completed across two decades, beginning in earnest in the 1880s and finalised in the first decade of this century, the project amounted to some fifty miles of quadruple main line, a significant achievement for any railway company anywhere. The route was further distinguished by the construction of several flyovers for ease of access on and off the main line, as for the Hampton Court line, and at Pirbright Junction, for Aldershot services.

Battledown Flyover, west of Basingstoke, marked the physical divergence of the Bournemouth line from that of the West of England route to Exeter. Access to each of these routes was made at Worting Junction from where the Bournemouth – Waterloo 'up' trains, crossed over the double tracks curving away westward to Andover on their way to Devon and Cornwall.

Battledown Flyover and the quadrupling work between Worting Junction and Basingstoke was completed and opened for 30 May 1897. Running south-westward, on favourable gradients for just under six miles, the line reached Lichfield Tunnel marking the commencement of a long 22 mile descent through the spectacular chalk downs with a ruling gradient of 1 in 252. Loops were also provided at Micheldelver and at Waller's Ash to maintain swift movement and schedules. Passing Winchester and Eastleigh where the London South Western established its Works in 1909, the line reached level ground at St Denys where the magnificent station of 1866 was incorporated in a rebuilding programme by the *LSWR* in 1899. St Denys was the meeting place with the coastal route to Fareham and Portsmouth. Separate platforms were provided for the Waterloo and Fareham coastal traffic, but retaining the 1866 station building on the 'up' Waterloo line. The St Denys-Fareham route was doubled in 1910/11. Two miles of level running led into Southampton. Quadruple track (May 1902) from St Denys to Northam Junction was in sharp contrast with the curves and confines of the final section into Southampton West (Central from 1935). At Northam, the original 1840 route ran straight into the terminus, whereas the later curve, giving a direct link from the line onto the 1847 Southampton-Dorchester line, was opened in 1858. Northam Curve imposed severe speed restrictions for this otherwise superb trunk route; it also bore witness to the fact that the original line of 1840 did not intend any advance westward. The terminus was decisive, but the role of the city's West station grew with the community itself. Extensive rebuilding here, (1931), together with massive investment at that time in dock development brought great change to the area, not least the land reclamation, putting the station someway inland, distanced from its former waterside setting. Further level sections west of Southampton through Millbrook, Redbridge – junction for Romsey, Salisbury and Andover – and Totton led out into the New Forest district, considered earlier in this overall survey.

A fine view of Bournemouth's premier train in the later 1950s. 'Merchant Navy' No 35018 *British India Line* is seen here approaching Basingstoke with the 'down' service on August Bank Holiday. 4 August 1958.                    *M. Mensing*

An intrinsic part of the improvements in civil engineering giving the Southern high performance service was that of the enlargement of specific, strategic stations. Basingstoke, for example, played a vital role as a veritable crossroads for Southern Railway services, north, south, east and west of the town. The quadrupling from Waterloo has been considered, likewise, the two routes to the south and west. Basingstoke also received and despatched trains from and to the Great Western Railway northward to Reading and, thereafter, the Midlands, North-West and the North-East of England.

Rebuilding of Basingstoke station and provision of new goods and locomotive sheds was well in excess of £100,000. Goods and locomotive premises were resited to the west of the station, as opposed to the former position to the east, whilst the former two platform provision with bays was transformed to give the town a prestigious new station incorporating four through platforms with an 'up' and 'down' bay. A three-storey main building on the 'down' side comprised the booking hall on the ground floor and access to an enamelled brick subway with lifts and stairs to the platforms. A feature of the new down platform, with its waiting rooms, refreshment and dining areas, offices and the like was the provision of a continuous covered roof. The island platform was fitted with a verandah roof. Steam heating was installed through-out the entire premises with a plan also to light the station completely by electricity. There was only limited change at the adjacent Great Western station. The main feature here was an upgrading of the junction with the Great Western line to and from Reading, reflecting the increased volume of cross-country services from the Midlands and the North of England. For access to the West Hampshire and Dorset resorts, and, indeed, for the entire West Country network of the *LSWR* and the later Southern Railway, Basingstoke fulfilled a similar function and strategic significance as that of Taunton on the Great Western Railway. Both locations served as vital gateways for traffic from London and from the Midlands and northern counties. The rebuilding work at Basingstoke was completed for December 1904.

Very different in association and imagery from exclusive services like *The Bournemouth Belle* were the Southern Railway Camping Coaches, introduced in 1935. First exhibited at Waterloo in February that year, the camping coaches went into service during that season. From 1 April to 30 June the charges were 50 shillings per week; from 1 July to 30 September, the amount rose to 70 shillings per week. The minimum requirement to rent the coaches was the purchase of four Monthly Return Tickets. Twelve coaches were provided for the first season, the majority going to the West Country – Cornwall and Devon. Hurn was the only site chosen in Hampshire. Southern publicity in the company magazine included the following statement:

The coaches are veritable bungalows on wheels. Their equipment includes everything necessary for the accommodation of six persons, even to a tin opener and cork screw. Wireless aerials also form part of their equipment.

The coaches themselves are divided into three separate compartments, comprising a living room, a compact little kitchen and sleeping accommodation for six people with wash basins in the sleeping compartments. Water is obtained from a 50 gallon tank under the coach with the necessary pumping apparatus to supply the kitchen tap.

For the 1937 season, the number of coaches had been increased, the locations for Hampshire and Dorset being Lyndhurst Road and Wool. Camping coaches were also sited at Tattenham Corner that year in connection with the Coronation. In the 1939 season coaches were provided at Hinton Admiral, Lyndhurst Road, and at Wool (for Lulworth Cove and Corfe Castle) in Dorset. There were also two classes of accommodation. An 'A' Class coach cost £3 during April, May, June and October and £4 per week during July, August and September. A 'B' Class coach cost £2.10s and £3.10s respectively. Both classes provided similar accommodation, but 'A' class was larger. The holiday atmosphere of the camping coach can lead us at this stage, into the specific subject of organised publicity and promotional works; a vital area.

Winchester on 24 April 1957 sees 'Battle of Britain' Light Pacific No 34109 *Sir Trafford Leigh Mallory* returning from the coast at the head of an 'up' Bournemouth-Waterloo service comprising a well kept set of Bulleid coaching stock.
*R.C. Riley*

Unrebuilt 'Merchant Navy' No 35012 *United States Line* races through Shawford Junction, south of Winchester with a 'down' Waterloo-Bournemouth/Weymouth express on 8 May 1955. The Didcot, Newbury and Southampton line of GWR association can be seen trailing in from the right. The GWR had its own station at Winchester. *R.C. Riley*

## Chapter Four
# THE SUNNY SOUTH COAST

Portsmouth and Southsea marked the eastern extremity of the *LSWR* coastal section, almost reaching the border with Sussex. Whereas Bournemouth had established a clearly defined specialist image as a holiday resort, Portsmouth and Southsea had a dual identity. Portsmouth had very close links with the military; Southsea, too. Naval traditions ran deep, and being host to the nation's principal naval dockyard with a distinguished maritime heritage reaching back over five centuries, tourism was but one element amongst many, albeit an important one. The twentieth century, however, had seen considerable development in tourism. By the late thirties Portsmouth, and especially Southsea, had much to offer as a holiday location.

Much of the active military presence on Southsea sea front had diminished by the thirties with the holiday trade in the ascendant. Southsea's magnificent Common was opened out with many attractions to sample. In the focal position between South Parade (1879) and Clarence Piers (1861) and adjoining the Common, an illuminated stepped Rock Garden was opened, likewise, a pleasure and activity complex including a miniature railway, boating pool, a swimming and paddling pool and tea gardens. A canoe lake with nearby gardens, tennis courts and putting green was also a feature to the east of South Parade Pier. The latter was rebuilt in 1908 to become the focus of the seafront attractions, being further developed between the Wars.

Three miles of sea front at Southsea, a significant attraction in itself, including Lumps Fort and Southsea Castle, were powerful reminders of the rich maritime heritage. Lumps Fort was purchased by the Corporation in 1931 and was developed as a further attraction, being landscaped as a garden setting with adjoining tennis courts and miniature golf. At the Dockyard, Nelson's flagship, *Victory*, the subject of patriotic poster work, added considerably to the historical dimension as, indeed, did the much earlier, and well known Roman fort on the 'Saxon Shore', at nearby Portchester. A somewhat 'later' Saxon church was added within the Roman walls, together with an imposing Norman Keep, thereby reflecting both historical continuity and change. In the City of Portsmouth itself, there was also the birthplace of Charles Dickens. His link with the city was commemorated in the Dickens Museum, his home, in Commercial Road.

Portsdown Hill, to the north of the city, offered a very different experience from that of the seafront, the maritime traditions, and indeed, the crowds anxious to promenade spectacle. Once there, up amongst the silent forts, the open space, Hampshire hinterland to the north, the panorama seaward, city far below, and Isle of Wight beyond, the 'Hill' revealed its magical quality.

The shifting moods and perspectives of time of day, of weather and the turn of the season, made this a special place, an experience more than a visit. The *Ward Lock Guide* for 1933 reflected this through a powerfully evocative piece of writing, drawing upon close observation, rich atmosphere and contrast:

It is a view of unceasing and ever changing charm; a view that, for all its evidence of the works of man, yet responds to every trick of wind and light and every condition of the tide. At 'full ebb' the great harbour is to a great extent 'high', if not actually 'dry'; but watch the returning waters as they fill each creek and pool, and one by one set afloat the stranded fishing boats with their drooping masts. Or come at dusk, when a golden haze in the west marks the path of the departed sun and watch how the dimness of the land becomes streaked with the long rows of lamps, how the apparently deserted harbour suddenly reawakens to life as a thousand lanterns are lit. Out in Spithead flickering buoys begin to twinkle, the forts take up the game which is repeated at a hundred points on the Isle of Wight, and then, to the accompaniment of a million twinkling lights, perhaps one of the great ocean liners will make its way down to the sea, itself invisible, but its myriad portholes spreading a golden sheen over the calm water.

For those of perhaps less aesthetic inclination but with a flair for activity and excitement, there was the racecourse at Paulsgrove, between Cosham and Portchester. Paulsgrove Halt served the racecourse directly; it opened on 28 June 1933 and closed with the onset of war in September 1939.

By way of final reference to Portsmouth itself, again sampling something of the definitive character of leisure in the mid and later thirties, we can focus on the newly opened Hilsea Lido. *Hints for Holidays*, 1939, devoted considerable space to this latest asset, built on the site of old fortifications:

Hilsea Lido is all that a modern and up-to-date open air swimming pool should be. It is 220 feet long, 60 feet broad and has a depth varying from 2 feet 6 inches for children to 15 feet for high diving. The water is aerated by cascades at each end of the pool ... One of the most important features of this splendid bath from a purely competitive point of view is the diving tower, which is the only one south of London to conform with the revised regulations of the English Diving Association.

There is dressing accommodation for 768 men and women and 189 children with emergency accommodation for many more and room for 1000 spectators, for whom deck chairs are provided. Spacious sun bathing accommodation, a compound for physical training, floodlighting by night, a large car park, loudspeakers, a children's paddling pool, and cafes for bathers and spectators, complete with amenities.

The Lido is a great success with residents and visitors alike.

Another great success for the progressive image of both Portsmouth and Southsea and the Southern Railway was the electrification programme inaugurating fast and efficient electric trains between London and the South Coast. Full electric services between Waterloo and Portsmouth on the 'Direct' line via Guildford began on 4 July 1937. One year later, on 2 July 1938, the 'Mid Sussex' route to Portsmouth on the former London Brighton and South Coast Railway was also electrified.

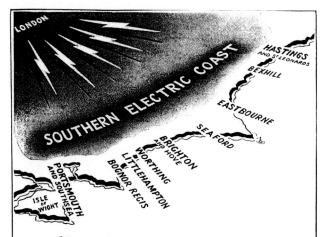

## Six Years' Progress

On JANUARY 1st, 1933, the first electrified Main Line Service in this country was introduced by the Southern Railway between London and Brighton and Worthing. Since then Eastbourne, Seaford, Bexhill, St. Leonards, Hastings, Portsmouth and Southsea, and Portsmouth Harbour (for the Isle of Wight) have been added to the holiday areas served by the Southern Electric.

In July, 1938, Littlehampton and Bognor Regis were added, thus transforming the whole of the South Coast between Hastings and Portsmouth into the "Southern Electric Coast."

The total mileage involved in these schemes amounts to 261 route miles, and the cost approximately £10,275,000.

*Top:* Guildford and the Portsmouth Direct Line on the eve of war. A very busy scene with three Waterloo-bound services on 11 August 1939. The Four-Cor Units comprise the express service from Portsmouth Harbour to Waterloo and are flanked by a 2 BIL unit, headcode 21, and an early LSWR set, No. 1206. The progressive 'Electric Coast' imagery of the late 1930s did much for the Southern's reputation as a modern, efficient railway.                          *F.E. Box*

*Opposite: Hints for Holidays,* 1939.

Portsmouth and Southsea now marked the western limit of what the Southern Railway proudly promoted as 'Southern Electric Coast'. The new electric trains also played an important role in promoting services to the Isle of Wight, Portsmouth Harbour being the principal departure point for the 'Island'.

According to *Seaside Watering Places*, 1904, there were 'few places more celebrated and praised for the beauty of both inland and coastal scenery than the Isle of Wight; It was 'England's Garden Isle' according to the Southern's *Hints for Holidays*, 1931, where E.P. Leigh-Bennett called it a 'Gem of the English Channel ... having all the natural charms for a perfect holiday island'. Elsewhere, S P B Mais, well known in Southern Railway circles, wrote of it in the preface to *Isles of the Island*, 1934:

I like the Isle of Wight because it is a delightful chunk of the Garden of England that has drifted far enough away to make it an island on its own.

Mais offered potent images of the 'Garden Isle', focussing upon the rich variety of landscape and experience, the appeal of past and present, and above all, atmosphere and character:

Isle of Wight villages are cosy, compact places with whitewashed thatched cottages and grey-towered Medieval churches. The Isle of Wight summer resorts, Ryde, Ventnor, Sea View, Sandown, Shanklin, Totland Bay, Yarmouth and the rest are cheerful places open to the sun, with miles of sands, and every opportunity for vigorous youth to take the sort of exercise that vigorous youth most likes.

But what I like best about the Isle of Wight is not Alum Bay with its multi-coloured cliffs, nor the pure white razor edge of the Needles, nor the fact that Tennyson and Queen Victoria lived there, and Charles I was imprisoned there, nor even Cowes regatta, that pageant of unforgettable beauty: but the chalked down of Arreton, Mersley and Ashley above Ryde where I have lain through a long summer afternoon with the smell of wild June roses mingling with the scent of wild thyme, and watched the slow steady procession of transatlantic liners entering Spithead, the white excursion steamers from Bournemouth and Brighton, and hundreds of small craft running into and out of Southampton Water as if they were bees at the entrance of a hive.

Ryde was the main gateway to the Island, and in the early days of tourism, *Seaside Watering Places*, 1904, took a very positive line. Immediately opposite Portsmouth and Southsea, a thirty-minute steamer trip, Ryde was noted as the 'largest town and most fashionable watering place'. Special attention was given to 'the many fine buildings mingled with a profusion of trees', likewise, to the fact that, 'the principal streets are wide, clean and well paved', and that the town was 'well supplied with good shops, hotels and lodging houses'.

From the earliest development as a resort, Ryde owed a great deal to its pier, 'the making of the place' as Ward Lock, 1909, put it. At nearly half a mile in length and comprising three sections – a promenade, the original dating back as early as 1814, with extension in 1833, a tramway section dating from 1864 and the Railway Pier, opened in July 1880, and owned jointly by the London and South Western and the London Brighton and South Coast Railways.

A magnificent period piece of Edwardian England. The beach at Sandown, Isle of Wight, in 1907. Note the large number of bathing machines near the water, beneath the Pier.

'Modern' Sandown as in 1937. The view of the beach and shoreline from the Pier. The progress and change over the previous thirty years is more than obvious, giving the atmosphere and character that prevailed into the sixties.

On the 'Western Wight', The Needles and their famous lighthouse framed by pine trees at Alum Bay. Freshwater was the railway's point of access to this superb landscape.

A view of the celebrated Seaview Suspension Pier as seen here in June 1949. Between Ryde and Bembridge the pier served steamers calling from South Parade and Clarence piers, at Portsmouth, likewise "excursionists from Bournemouth and Southampton". The pier reached some thousand feet from the shore and could accommodate three ships alongside. Of Seaview itself, the Ward-Lock guide for 1909 commented: "There is a welcome absence of bustle about the place – it looks what it is, a spot for idleness and quiet enjoyment".

Ward Lock offered an historical note:

It is interesting to recall that Ryde Pier was one of the first institutions of the kind in the country and at one time enjoyed a reputation almost as unique as that of the old Chain Pier at Brighton.

Before the rise of the numerous watering places that now girdle our coasts, Ryde was a chosen resort of the elite, and dukes and earls took the air on the pier as systematically as they and their imitation now take the waters at Homburg and Marienbad. The large family mansions in various parts of the town remain as memorial to a departed and almost forgotten era in Ryde's history.

The pier-head was further improved in 1895 with the construction of the dome-shaped Pavillion incorporating a concert-hall for 1000 people, adjoining refreshment and reading rooms, and, nearby, the accompanying premises of the Royal Victoria Yacht Club. The later Victorian Pier, dating from 1859, a more modest affair and much shorter, became a useful bathing place.

Ryde Esplandade was also the subject of much approval. Developed from reclaimed mud flats the area east of the Esplanade station made a great contribution to the holiday image at Ryde. By the thirties this area included a Pavillion, (at a point adjacent to the railway tunnel leading out to St John's Road station) canoe lake and the bowling and putting greens of Ashley and Sandringham Gardens. Hints for Holidays noted that the putting greens and lake were floodlit at night. Further east was the coastal walk to Seaview passing the picturesque ivy-covered Appley Tower on the shore itself. Puckpool Park given the prefix 'famous' in Hints for Holidays was a development dating from 1928. In that year, St Helen's Urban District Council transformed the old gun battery site into a pleasure ground comprising tennis courts, putting greens bowling greens, refreshment facilities, woodland walks and, of course, bathing huts to emphasise the seashore, the prime objective of many visitors to the Island.

Progressive investment in the community was certain to create the desired effect. This policy can be traced back to the initial stages of tourist activity. Concern for adequate standards of public health – water supply, sewerage schemes etc – were definitive of early priorities and essential to the overall character, association and image of the resorts.

Annual statements from the Local Government Board indicated early levels of investment. For 1873/74 and the Third Annual Report, Ryde spent £1,440 on improving public health: for the same year, Sandown returned a figure of £477 and Shanklin £1,007 on sewerage schemes. At Ventnor £2,300 was invested for the purchase of land and for extension of the esplanade; the commitment here by the end of 1875 amounted to over £8,000. Returns for 1878/79 revealed that Sandown spent £1,477 on pleasure grounds and £3,450 on sewerage schemes; likewise, Shanklin, with an expenditure of £2,415 on extensions to the esplanade and £1,341 on the installation of groynes and sewerage outfalls The Eleventh Annual Report for 1881/82 records that at Ryde £2,500 was spent on sewerage works, £7,193 on developing the water supply and £3,000 on the extension of the esplandade, public walks and pleasure gardens. Investments such as these were vital to the overall expansion of tourism on the Island, which, by the twentieth century, had become pre-eminent. Ryde,

Sandown, Shanklin and Ventnor, all served by the Isle of Wight Railway Company, were the major tourist attractions as the investment record here shows. This, of course, was all good news for that particular railway company which, not surprisingly, was the busiest, most profitable of the Island's network, this century.

Together with the obvious attractions of the Island's hinterland, Carisbrooke Castle and Osborne House, beloved of Queen Victoria, offered historical and cultural dimensions. Osborne was a particular favourite with all its associations of royalty and tradition. First opened to the public in May 1904, it attracted an average of 60,000 people annually during the decade up to the First World War. Whilst inland landscape and historical locations undoubtedly added to the rich variety of experience that defined the Isle of Wight, it was the coastal resorts that made the greatest impact, however.

Visitors to Shanklin, for example, were well advised by Hints for Holidays to ensure an early booking for the months July to September, such was the popularity of the resort. Like its twin and neighbour, Sandown, Shanklin faced south east, 'a town on the cliffs', and was noted for its famous Chine, its gardens and the cliff and seashore walks. As Hints for Holidays would have it:

In whichever way one strolls there are new beauties to please the mind and keep the eye alert.

Shanklin Chine was further enhanced by the famous Rylstone Gardens. S P B Mais, in Isle of the Island, recognised the definitive nature of these formations for the Isles of Wight"

Chines are to the Isle of Wight what cream is to Devon, something rich and rare, and unobtainable in quite the same form elsewhere. They are deep, green ravines with tumbling waters, crossed by ornamental foot-bridges and overhung with trees and giant ferns.

Hints for Holidays presented Shanklin as a sylvan paradise:

The title 'Leafy Shanklin' gives only a hint of the loveliness of this beautiful resort. Its refreshing leafiness is one of its main characteristics, the whole district being a picture of foliage and flowers from early spring to late autumn. Shanklin is famous for its magnificent hydrangeas, and noble trees provide a canopy in the lanes, the chines, and the dells. Flowers bloom in rich profusion – primroses and bluebells in the woods, crimson and pink valerian on the rocky banks, honeysuckle in the hedges, hydrangeas and roses in the gardens.

Earlier, in 1913, Winter Resorts in the Homeland had stressed the attractions and associations of climate and location with regard to Ventnor:

Ventnor is pre-eminent in the heart of the lovely undercliff district. The mildness of its winter climate is such that sub-tropical plants flourish out of doors. The position of the town on the terraced slopes of the Downs which rise to 800ft, within little more than half a mile form the sea, has earned it the title, 'Malvern by the Sea'.

'The Western Wight', 'Tennyson's Country', provided a somewhat different atmosphere from the well known and much visited eastern resorts. Being somewhat more remote it was praised for its rural character and magnificent coastal location. Alum Bay, Freshwater and Yarmouth were the main settlements here. Alum Bay, famous for its coloured sands, also offered a chine and

The Old Village, Shanklin, Isle of Wight.    564.

GODSHILL CHURCH. I.O.W.                    L 539

*Top and left:* Two very different images of the Island, focussing on its rural, traditional character but of the same period are those of Shanklin's 'Old Village', as opposed to the bolder new resort town, and that of Godshill Church, with attendant thatched buildings.

*Opposite left:* Pine Walk, in the early years of this century. Famous for its chines and, certainly, its pines, Bournemouth captilised on the healthy, positive imagery and associations involved. 'The Pines Express' was the railways own manner of celebration, adding to the exclusive, distinguished character of the resort nationally.

the opportunity to wander the cliffs in sight of the spectacular Needles formation and their lighthouse, one of the definitive landscapes of England. Freshwater Bay was given the identity "Ozoneville" at the turn of the century. In contrast with the busier more developed, resorts across the Island, one writer at the time, observed that what it lacked in "gorgeous piers and esplanades", it more than compensated for it its "natural restfulness".

S P B Mais, Leigh-Bennett and, indeed, the entire thrust of Southern Railway publicity, stressed the accessibility of the Isle of Wight whilst at the same time celebrating its island image and status. According to Mais:

> You can cross to it from the mainland in about twenty minutes. It is much too large for a single man to own, but is just the right size to cope with a summer invasion. I have been all round it in much less than a single day, for the excursion on that occasion started from Brighton at eight o'clock in the morning and by eight o'clock in the evening we were in Brighton again.

Looking at the nature and achievement of Southern Railway promotional work, there was much to be admired. From the ultra-modern 'Electric Coast', the delights of the 'Garden Island', the experience of 'Historic Exeter', or the remote grandeur of the legendary landscapes of North Cornwall, the company presented itself as one ideally placed to combine choice of resort, manner and mood, with the highest standards of service. The Solent and its wider surrounding area more than fulfilled the various hopes and expectations of those holidaying on the Southern's 'Sunny South Coast'.

Returning now, from the Island to the mainland it was clear that Bournemouth was an extremely prestigious resort for the Southern Railway. It enjoyed something of a national rather than regional reputation given the wide-ranging train services from many parts of Britain, not least, the Midlands and the North, via the Somerset and Dorset Railway. Likewise, the main line from Waterloo and the cross-country routes from the Midlands via Basingstoke, and South Wales, via Salisbury, helped establish Bournemouth as one of Britain's leading resorts. *The Bournemouth Belle* from Waterloo and *The Pines Express* from Manchester reflected the status of the resort.

LMS publicity work made much of Bournemouth. The Company took a substantially different format and focus in its famous *Holidays By LMS* than that of the other three companies. Whereas the others, *Holiday Haunts*, *Hints for Holidays* and *The Holiday Handbook* celebrated their own resorts, almost exclusively, *Holidays By LMS* went for national coverage and the pivotal role of the company in Britain's holiday trade, overall. Bournemouth and the South Coast generally could only benefit from the extensive links with the Midlands and the North. Full-page advertisements for the resort brought it, and the LMS, into close identity.

Since the early years of this century, Bournemouth had developed a distinctive image based on certain, undoubted, attractions. The town became famous for its chines, its extensive parks and gardens, and for the range and quality of its amenities as a stylish, successful resort. It was a triumph of civic enterprise.

*Hints for Holidays*, 1939, ever anxious to celebrate the attractions at Bournemouth praised the parks and gardens:

> It is estimated that within the Borough of Bournemouth alone there are over one hundred miles of drives and footpaths, through the gardens, beautiful parks, picturesque chines,

PINE WALK BOURNEMOUTH.

# L M S
## THROUGH TRAINS
between

MANCHESTER          LIVERPOOL
(LONDON ROAD).          (LIME STREET).

NOTTINGHAM,          LEICESTER

BIRMINGHAM, ETC.

with connections from principal
: : LMS Stations in the : :

NORTH AND MIDLANDS

and

# BOURNEMOUTH
(WEST)

with connections for

SOUTHAMPTON, PORTSMOUTH,
SWANAGE, WEYMOUTH, ETC.

*For train times, etc., apply at any LMS Station, Office or Agency.*

Bournemouth Pier on a sunny summer's afternoon during the 1920s. Opened in August 1880 by the Lord Mayor of London, no less, the pier became a focal centre for leisure and entertainment, a definitive feature of the town's special character. Note the wooded, parkland approach to the Pier and seashore, adding to the favourable imagery and impact.

extensive pinewoods and moorlands and along the magnificent sea front and cliffs.

The guide books took every opportunity to stress the luxuriant imagery and association expected of a distinguished resort and the gardens made a significant contribution here. The Ward Lock guide of 1934 gave details:

Palms flourish in the gardens and thickets of bamboo. In their season camellias and azaleas vie with rhododendron, magnolias, genista, and guelder rose. The flowering cherry, the pyrus and the Mexican orange alternate with the lovely ceanothus, or the flowering currant with white and yellow broom. Berberis of choice variety contrast with graceful silver birch, or shining copper beech or many others whose names would fill a page.

Sports and leisure facilities made for a positive litany of delight:

Added to the wonderfully varied scenery of this land of pines and sunshine is the opportunity of constantly changing recreation, the facilities for golfing, fishing, shooting, hunting, cricket, tennis, bowls, croquet, boating and other outdoor pastimes being un-equalled at any resort in Britain.

Seafront attractions were far from the bland, featureless developments said to characterise many resorts. *Hints for Holidays* was quick to reassure its readers:

The fine Undercliff Drive Promenade now extends from Alum Chine to Southbourne, a distance of about five miles, and the Overcliff Drive to the east and west afford pleasant alternatives, still more extensive. The chines are picturesque

ravines or miniature valleys, which break up the cliffs into unique and exceptionally interesting formations.

The East Undercliff extending between the piers – Bournemouth and Boscombe – led the visitor from the former to the latter community. Anxious to develop and sustain its own identity, Boscombe had its Chine Gardens leading inward from the pier, making an excellent access to and from the seashore. The shoreline itself was also a considerable attraction.

Like Bournemouth, Boscombe grew rapidly, its surrounding area experiencing an obvious transformation. This was something worth the mention by Ward Lock in its 1933 edition, Bournemouth:

In its earliest days Boscombe consisted of a few dilapidated cottages whose dwellers found employment in a neighbouring brickfield, and refreshment in an inn - rural but uninviting. As if by the touch of a magic hand, stately hotels took the place of the public house; pleasant villas, surrounded by gardens and tree-shaded, arose where mud cottages once stood; and where the men of not very ancient Boscombe laboured in the brickfields, people now saunter along the lovely Chine Gardens which take high rank among the lovely corners of this delightful coast.

Boscombe has its own Pier, its own Pleasure Gardens, and possesses almost every feature which goes to the making of an independent watering place; yet it is but a part of the great Bournemouth family.

Bournemouth took special pride in possessing the largest Municipal Orchestra in the world. Performances were given throughout the year in the Municipal

This early 1960s view eastward towards Bournemouth Pier illustrates another practical function of the Pier, namely access to the steamers that plied the coastal waters here. Regular trips to and from Bournemouth, to Swanage, Weymouth, Southampton docks and the Isle of Wight broadened the appeal of the resort.

Alum Chine, looking east towards Bournemouth Pier. This view from 1935 shows the development and extent of the promenade and shoreline by this time.

Pavillion, opened in 1929 at a cost in excess of a quarter of a million pounds, did much to enhance the image of the resort as a cultural centre. Four theatres, 'numerous first-class cinemas' and a newly opened (1937) indoor swimming pool, likewise, added to the favourable image and helped to promote Bournemouth as a winter resort also. *Hints for Holidays* considered Bournemouth to have special appeal for winter holidays. The pineland imagery celebrating the fact that Bournemouth claimed a million pine trees locally, was a definite asset, and the basis for the aptly named *Pines Express* mentioned earlier. The link with Manchester and, therefore, the North Country was also a statement of contrast, promoting 'Southern Sunshine'. Railway poster-work exploited this creatively.

Given the pier, the chines, gardens and the numerous leisure, sporting and cultural amenities, Bournemouth made a powerful appeal to middle-class expectations.

This much was clear in the pages of *Hints for Holidays*:

The majority of the hotels and boarding houses are situated in their own grounds amid the pines in lovely nooks and corners of the Evergreen Valley.

Together with its own specific attractions, Bournemouth also served as an ideal centre from which visitors could explore the wider district. The New Forest and Corfe Castle, in nearby Dorset, offered outstanding experience of landscape and history. *Walking at Weekends* by S P B Mais and published by the Southern Railway, included three guided walks through the New Forest. Mais recommended Brockenhurst: 'the best centre by far to explore the New Forest'. Looking seaward, there were many excursions east and west along the coast and to the Isle of Wight. Excursions from Bournemouth Pier ventured as far west as Torquay, eastward to Brighton and across the Channel to Jersey, Guernsey and to Cherbourg. Southampton, Portsmouth, Swanage and Weymouth were regular destinations, whilst voyages around the Isle of Wight and to specific resorts – Ryde, Shanklin, Yarmouth, Totland Bay and Cowes – linked with roads and railways to visit inland

The London and South Western and the later Southern Railway made much of the close association and identity between their railway services and the magnificent spectacle of the New Forest. No opportunity was lost to celebrate this outstanding asset. J. Thornton Burge on behalf of *LSW* promotional interests underlined that particular relationship:

The London and South Western Railway is unique in being the only railway which directly serves the New Forest. The district is one of the most beautiful in England and is within easy reach, not only of London, Southampton and Portsmouth, but also of large centres in the Midlands and the North of England.

The main line of the London and South Western Railway to Bournemouth and to Weymouth runs through the New Forest, while the line from Salisbury to Wimborne, via West Moors skirts its western boundaries. The London and South Western stations within its area on the Bournemouth Main Line are Lyndhurst Road, Brockenhurst, and Holmsley, while Lymington, Sway, Hinton, Admiral, Christchurch, Hurn and Ringwood are on its outskirts. On the West Moors Branch, Daggens Road, Fordingbridge and Breamore are the nearest stations to the Forest. The nearest other railway to the New Forest is the Great Western Railway at Winchester and Salisbury.

The final sentence was decisive in its brevity.

Bournemouth made an excellent centre for access to the Forest district, offering a valuable alternative to the bustle of the modern resort and to things maritime. The New Forest was always an historical as well as aesthetic experience: it also offered superb walking. S P B Mais, included three new Forest Walks in his *Walking at Weekends* published by the Southern itself.

Lymington and Brockenhurst were popular destinations for local visits as well as for excursions from further afield. Looking at the journey westward into the Forest, Thornton Burge gave details on Lyndhurst, its station and traffic:

After leaving Southampton the London and South Western Railway's main line enters the New Forest

# THROUGH EXPRESS TRAINS
## BETWEEN
## BOURNEMOUTH, SOUTHAMPTON, WINCHESTER, BIRMINGHAM, MANCHESTER, &c.,
RUN AS UNDER
### EVERY WEEK DAY
### until further notice.
### (BANK HOLIDAYS EXCEPTED).

Connections to and from Portsmouth, the Isle of Wight, Swanage, &c.

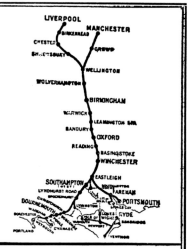

## FROM SOUTH TO NORTH
(First and Third Classes only.)

| Station | a.m. | a.m. |
|---|---|---|
| SWANAGE (Join Thro' Train at Bournemouth Cent.) dep. | 8 58 | 10 11 |
| BOURNEMOUTH { West " | 10 15 | 11 20 |
| { Central " | 10 25 | 11 31 |
| Boscombe " | 10 29 | 11 36 |
| Yarmouth, I.W. (Via Lymington) " | 9 0 | 10B15 |
| Lymington Town " | 9A36 | 10B56 |
| | | p.m. |
| Brockenhurst " | 10A39 | 12 2 |
| SOUTHAMPTON WEST " | 11 10 | 12 23 |
| EASTLEIGH arr. | 11 21 | 12 33 |
| | a.m. | a.m. |
| Cowes (via Southampton) dep. | 7 15 | 9 50 |
| SOTHMPTN. TN. (for Docks) " | 10 24 | 11 58 |
| | | p.m. |
| Eastleigh arr. | 10 41 | 12 15 |
| Ryde Pier Head (via Portsmouth) dep. | 8 50 | 10 10 |
| Portsmouth Harbour " | 9 30 | 10 45 |
| Portsmouth (Town) " | 9 35 | 10 50 |
| Fratton & Southsea " | 9 39 | 10 55 |
| Eastleigh arr. | 10 27 | 11 41 |
| Stokes Bay dep. | 9 30 | 10 50 |
| Gosport Road and Alverstoke " | 9 34 | 10 54 |
| Gosport " | 9 40 | 11 0 |
| Fareham " | 10 5 | 11 21 |
| Eastleigh arr. | 10 27 | 11 41 |
| | | p.m. |
| EASTLEIGH dep. | 11 25 | 12 36 |
| WINCHESTER " | ... | 12 51 |
| BASINGSTOKE arr. | ... | 1 21 |
| | p.m. | |
| BASINGSTOKE dep. | | 1 25 |
| READING (West) arr. | ... | 1 48 |
| OXFORD " | 12 55 | 2 34 |
| BANBURY " | ... | 3 22 |
| RUGBY arr. | ... | 4 5 |
| LEICESTER (Central) " | ... | 4 28 |
| NOTTINGHAM (Victoria) " | ... | 5 3 |
| SHEFFIELD (Victoria) " | ... | 5 56 |
| LEAMINGTON SPA arr | 1 50 | ... |
| BIRMINGHAM (Snow Hill) " | 2 25 | ... |
| WOLVERHAMPTON (Low Level) " | 2 47 | ... |
| CREWE arr. | 3 55 | ... |
| STOCKPORT " | 4 36 | 8 25 |
| MANCHESTER (London Road) " | 4 50 | 7G25 |
| BRADFORD " | ... | 8 32 |
| YORK " | ... | 7 37 |
| NEWCASTLE " | ... | 10P16 |
| SHREWSBURY arr. | 3 41 | ... |
| Gobowen " | 5 52 | ... |
| Oswestry " | 6 13 | ... |
| RUABON " | 4 27 | ... |
| WREXHAM " | 4 39 | ... |
| CHESTER " | 4 57 | ... |
| Warrington (Leave Through Train at Chester) " | 5 50 | ... |
| BIRKENHEAD (Woodside) " | 5 35 | ... |
| LIVERPOOL { Central " | 5K40 | ... |
| { Landing Stage " | 5 47 | ... |

(vertical side notes: Join Through Train at Eastleigh. — Restaurant Car Express Bournemouth and Southampton to Sheffield, Manchester, Bradford, and York.)

## FROM NORTH TO SOUTH
(First and Third Classes only.)

| Station | a.m. | a.m. |
|---|---|---|
| LIVERPOOL { Landing Stage dep. | 9 30 | ... |
| { Central " | 9L33 | ... |
| BIRKENHEAD (Woodside) " | 9 45 | ... |
| Warrington (Join Through Train at Chester) " | 9 5 | ... |
| CHESTER " | 10 20 | ... |
| WREXHAM " | 10 41 | ... |
| RUABON " | 10 17 | ... |
| Oswestry " | 10 15 | ... |
| GOBOWEN " | 10 31 | ... |
| SHREWSBURY " | 11 21 | ... |
| MANCHESTER (London Road) dep. | 10 15 | 10M0 |
| STOCKPORT " | 10 25 | ... |
| CREWE " | 11 8 | ... |
| | p.m. | |
| WOLVERHAMPTON (Low Level) dep. | 12 16 | ... |
| BIRMINGHAM (Snow Hill) " | 12 39 | ... |
| LEAMINGTON SPA " | 1 12 | ... |
| | a.m. | |
| NEWCASTLE dep. | ... | 8 0 |
| YORK " | ... | 10 23 |
| BRADFORD (Exchange) " | 7 20 | 10 0 |
| SHEFFIELD (Victoria) " | 9 36 | 11 21 |
| | | p.m. |
| NOTTINGHAM (Victoria) " | 10 28 | 12 27 |
| LEICESTER (Central) " | 10 58 | 1 1 |
| RUGBY " | 11 23 | 1 26 |
| BANBURY dep. | 1E22 | 2 2 |
| OXFORD " | 2 7 | 2 45 |
| READING (West) " | ... | 3 25 |
| BASINGSTOKE arr. | ... | 3 52 |
| BASINGSTOKE dep. | ... | 4 0 |
| WINCHESTER " | ... | 4 26 |
| EASTLEIGH " | 3 36 | 4 38 |
| Eastleigh dep. | 3 45 | 4 52 |
| Fareham arr. | 4 6 | 5 13 |
| Gosport " | 4 21 | 5 27 |
| Gosport Road and Alverstoke " | 5 9 | 6 32 |
| Stokes Bay " | 5 13 | 6 36 |
| Eastleigh dep. | 3 45 | 5 40 |
| Fratton & Southsea arr. | 4 32 | 6 29 |
| Portsmouth (Town) " | 4 37 | 6 35 |
| Portsmouth Harbour " | 4 42 | ... |
| Ryde Pier Head (via Portsmouth) " | 5 45 | 7N40 |
| Eastleigh dep. | 4 10 | 5 10 |
| SOTHMPTN. TN. (for Docks) arr. | 4 27 | 5 27 |
| Cowes West Pier (via S'thamp'n) " | ... | 6 55 |
| EASTLEIGH dep. | 3 39 | 4 41 |
| SOUTHAMPTON WEST arr. | 3 50 | 4 52 |
| Brockenhurst " | 4F25 | 5 43 |
| Lymington Town " | 4 45 | 6 6 |
| Yarmouth, I.W. (via Lymington) " | 5 20 | 7 55 |
| Boscombe " | 4 31 | 5 49 |
| BOURNEMOUTH { Central " | 4 36 | 5 54 |
| { West " | 4 49 | 6 7 |
| SWANAGE " | 6C12 | 7B10 |

(vertical side notes: Leave Through Train at Eastleigh. — Restaurant Car Express York, Bradford, Manchester and Sheffield to Southampton and Bournemouth.)

A—Join Through Train at Southampton West.
B—Join Through Train at Brockenhurst.
C—Leave Through Train at Southampton West.
D—Leave Through Train at Bournemouth Central.
E—Join Through Train at Oxford.
F—Arrive 4.28 p.m. Saturdays.
G—Manchester Central (G.C.R.).
K—Leave through train at Rock Ferry.
L—Join through train at Rock Ferry.
M—Great Central Railway.
N—During June arrive Ryde 7.55 p.m.
P—During June arrive 10.50 p.m.

### RESTAURANT CAR TRAINS.
The times of other Companies' Trains shown hereon are subject to alteration for July. For particulars see respective Companies' Time Tables.

*LSWR* Timetable, 1914

at Lyndhurst Road, 88 miles from Waterloo and 11 miles from Southampton. Beautiful woods abound on all sides of the station and in summer as many as 5,000 children are conveyed to this station in a day from Southampton and other large centres for their school outings. At such times the accommodation is taxed to its utmost capacity. The station is situated on a very sharp curve at the eastern end of which there is a level crossing. There are two cross-over roads which admit of a train engine "running round" 22 coaches, but with very long trains in the summer months this is scarcely sufficient. The signal box is at the east end of the station and controls a level crossing of the main Southampton road over the railway at that point.

*Hints for Holidays* and, indeed, all travel guides recognised Lyndhurst as the 'Capital of the New Forest'. Although three miles from Lyndhurst Road station, 'the broad straight road runs through the Forest the whole distance ...'. There was regular transport to the town, but one was advised wherever possible to enjoy the splendid walk. Historical and aesthetic experience blended at Lyndhurst, with the ancient 'King Oak of Knightwood' measuring about 20 feet around and the site nearby of the Rufus Stone marking the forest location where William the Conqueror's son, William Rufus, was killed by an arrow. The entire forest, of course, derived its name and much of its character and appearance from the decision of William I, the Conqueror, to create the New Forest as his exclusive hunting domain.

There was yet more history in the form of Beaulieu Abbey, a Cistercian House close to the River Beaulieu itself. Beaulieu Road station, almost three miles south of Lyndhurst, across open heathscape, was the railway access to Beaulieu. A distance of 3½ miles separated the community itself from its station, and just over a mile beyond the latter, the line curved westward through woodland again, to Brockenhurst. S P B Mais considered Brockenhurst to be 'the best centre by far from which to explore the New Forest'. His winter walk, (part of the *Walking at Weekends* hand-book from the Southern Railway) from Brockenhurst to Beaulieu thence to Lymington showed how one could use the railway system to derive the best experience of the Forest area overall. His description of Beaulieu forms part of the walk, included here by way of reference.

Looking at Brockenhurst, its role as a centre for exploration was established by the early years of the century. Thornton Burge's essay 'The L and S W Railway in the New Forest District' considered this:

Brockenhurst as a centre for the New Forest increases in popularity year by year, and the village grows accordingly. This is evidenced by the fact that apart from the number of new houses, two new large residential hotels have been built and opened within the last seven years and are always well filled, as in addition to the summer visitors, the hunting in winter is a great attraction and families come from as far north as Scotland.

Nearer to home, it was also pointed out that Brockenhurst was a favourite location for excursion trains with large numbers of people arriving from Bournemouth as day visitors. Amongst these, school parties and Sunday School outings featured considerably. Upwards of 2000 people at a time visited Brockenhurst for such occasions. Thornton Burge drew attention to one particular event:

For many years a fete organised on behalf of the London and South Western Railway's Widows' and Orphans' Benefit Society has been held here and on these occasions some 5000 passengers are dealt with without any interference with the ordinary train services. Many of these passengers come from places as far remote as London and Exeter, all attracted by the unsurpassed beauties of the New Forest. For this purpose, the Company generously places special trains at the disposal of the Committee, very low fares being charged.

Brockenhurst was also the junction for the Lymington branch opened on 12 July 1858, over four miles to the town, and eventually, on 8 May 1884, to Lymington Quay where the ferry services crossed to the Isle of Wight at Yarmouth. Brockenhurst was also the starting point westward for the Bournemouth 'direct' line via Sway and Hinton Admiral. As considered earlier, the station was extensively rebuilt and enlarged in connection with the new line. Holmsley, on the original *LSWR* main line to Weymouth, was also a popular location for Forest visits. London and South Western publicity works stressed its attractions, not least, as part of a scenic journey by train. Considering the line between Holmsley and Ringwood we read:

The line here runs through a portion of the New Forest, and has a beauty all of its own: luxuriant trees, heather, fern and wild healthy moorland, with abundance of bird and animal life.

To the west of Bournemouth, Holes Bay Curve and the Branksome avoiding line were opened on 1 June 1893. The former made up the base of a triangular section leading along a causeway across the waters of Holes Bay, north-west of Poole to Hamworthy Junction, thereby eliminating the need to run northward to Broadstone in order to reverse for access westward. The Branksome avoiding line was a short link, again completing a triangular junction whereby trains travelling westward from Bournemouth avoided the reversal at Bournemouth West, by-passing it instead.

Once into rural Dorset, the line ran through the largely level heathland to historic Wareham where a new station was opened on 4 April 1887, in connection with the opening of the Swanage branch. There were two platforms, each 185 yards with both 'up' and 'down' bays. The Swanage branch opened on 20 May 1885 with one intermediate station, Corfe Castle, over the 10 mile line from Worgret Junction to the coast. Corfe Castle was yet another example of a community and landscape blending historical tradition with a very high degree of aesthetic excellence.

By this stage, the *LSWR* was well into that part of the county made famous as Thomas Hardy's 'Wessex' heartland. Wool, the next station, 18 miles from Bournemouth, and five miles west of Wareham, was the departure point for the road link to the famous Lulworth Cove and the spectacular chalk cliffs, formations such as Durdle-Dor sculpted by the eternal action of the sea. Lulworth Cove was a 5½ mile drive from Wool. Close by the station at Wool, south of the line, were the remains of Bindon Abbey, whilst immediately north, across the River Frome, was Wool Bridge House, both locations being used as settings in Thomas Hardy's famous work *Tess of the D'Urbervilles*.

From Wareham westward the line runs the distance to Dorchester through the Frome Valley, Hardy's 'Valley

Brockenhurst at a busy period on 11 September 1953. At the 'down' main line platform is the Birkenhead-Bournemouth hauled by 'Lord Nelson' 4-6-0 No 30864 *Sir Martin Frobisher* whilst the branch service for Lymington worked by 0-4-4T M7 Class No 30058 waits alongside. The GWR coaching stock in the sidings is that of the Sats New Milton-Swansea train.
R.C. Riley

A definitive photograph of the 1950s with *M.V. Lymington* at the slipway/pier at Lymington itself as seen on 26 August 1954. The vessel was introduced in 1938 and worked the crossing to Yarmouth until 1972.

*R.C. Riley*

of The Great Dairies'. Beyond Wool, the line passes Moreton station and, soon, the village of West Stafford before entering Dorchester South, and thence the junction with the Great Western Railway for the final stage over the steeply graded section, as severe as 1 in 50 in the 'up' direction, between Dorset's county town and Weymouth, 'The Royal Resort'. The sharp curve onto the Great Western line, and the isolated 'up' platform into which trains had to reverse, made for an obvious reminder of mid-century aspirations to push westward from Dorchester with a coastal route to Exeter. Southern Railway publicity celebrated the fact that their line between Dorchester South and Bournemouth offered direct access to the landscape of Thomas Hardy's novels and, of course, to Dorchester itself, Hardy's *Casterbridge*.

This outline survey of the various attractions open to tourists at Bournemouth – the resort itself and the surrounding districts – hopefully goes some way to explain the appeal of the place, and the fact that for the railway company there was no doubt of its position, not only as a major resort on the Southern Railway, but as one of Britain's most distinguished and widely visited locations. Bournemouth, unlike many English resorts, had a national character as well as local and regional popularity. Population figures for the early years have been given, but a longer perspective, taken over the period 1861-1931, is instructive:

| | | |
|------|---|---------|
| 1861 | – | 1707 |
| 1871 | – | 5896 |
| 1881 | – | 16,859 |
| 1901 | | |
| 1911 | – | 78,674 |
| 1921 | – | |
| 1931 | – | 116,797 |

Bournemouth's western neighbour, Poole, also felt the benefits of increased tourist activity. The borough boundaries, extended in 1905, took in the expanding eastward suburbs, where Branksome and Canford Cliffs rapidly assumed tourist and residential identity, reinforcing the associations of confidence, prosperity and progress. Poole, itself, was promoted by the Southern Railway as 'The Dorset Lakeland'. It offered that delightful combination of past and present. *Hints for Holidays* featured both:

There is the old-world atmosphere on and around historic Poole Quay, where the Fifteenth Century Town House and Guildhall, the remains of the medieval sea wall, the Town Cellars and numerous examples of Tudor and Georgian architecture will furnish a feast for all who take a delight in 'old walls, old roofs' and the sunlight upon them.

It also praised Branksome, like all other guides. Municipal interest at Branksome capitalised on the opportunity to create a stylish image, as distinguished in its appearance as that of neighbouring Bournemouth, and, like the latter, with the full advantage of favourable natural landscape. This was, indeed, the message clearly expressed in the *Ward Lock Guide* for the area in the early thirties. Looking at The Avenue, the principal thoroughfare southward to the sea, and to Branksome Chine, we read:

The Avenue, in June, with its wide banks of rhododendrons and flanking rows of pines, is more like a New Forest glade than a modern street...

A vital element of the Southern's holiday imagery was this successful marriage of aesthetics – landscape and tradition – with the best in modern amenities, especially active pursuits. It was a definitive feature of the period, by no means confined to Southern aspirations.

Beyond The Avenue at the shore was the access to Branksome Chine. Backing inland, the Chine embodied the holiday experience of the area. Details were in the *Ward Lock Guide* and in the Southern's *Hints for Holidays*.

The latter recorded that the local authority had recently purchased the land here. It also stressed that the new bathing station provided there had been the product of careful study of the Continental sun-bathing establishments. A Municipal Cafe with roof garden was also provided. The *Ward Lock Guide* continued:

A broad valley winding inland for nearly a mile, studded with fine trees and luxuriant with heather, bracken and rhododendrons. In its depths a stream winds towards the sea, and shady paths branch off in all directions revealing unexpected gems of scenery ... In its upper reaches are tennis courts and putting and bowling greens; its lower end pierces the cliffs and reveals a fine stretch of sands which is extremely popular. Recognising the need of providing for the crowds who come here for bathing, picnicking and other seaside delights, the Poole Corporation have built an extremely well equipped bathing-station with cafes, a sun-lounge and other such amenities. In addition to the cabins in the bathing-station there are numerous huts or day bungalows for hire, and there is also a Motor Park.

If the details, the character and style of these amenities were unmistakably period-piece, so, too, was the final reference to the motor-car. Its potential had not yet been pursued and long-term changes were inevitable, but for the inter-war years, and the decade or so after World War Two, the fortunes and the focus for the railways and the resorts remained inseparable.

In overview, the wide-ranging and intensive pattern of train services founded around the turn of the century and developed, thereafter, up to the Second World War, were vital to the growth and reputation of the South Coast resorts. During the post-war years, down to the early sixties, the essential structure and character of tourism, the resorts and their attendant train services, was maintained. The style, imagery and character of these resorts, and, indeed, the expectations of holiday-makers themselves, were not appreciably different from those of the late thirties. But from the mid-sixties onwards, the recognised pattern was broken. Detailed structural changes followed for railways and resorts alike posing serious questions for both their futures, as is all too evident today.

# CROSS COUNTRY SERVICES
## TO AND FROM THE
# SOUTH COAST RESORTS
*The whole journey without change!*

**SKETCH MAP** showing Route to and from FOLKESTONE, DOVER DEAL, RAMSGATE MARGATE, BRIGHTON EASTBOURNE HASTINGS, ETC. SOUTHAMPTON BOURNEMOUTH & ISLE OF WIGHT

Through Express Services are run by the G.W.R. between the following centres and South Coast Resorts, with connections to and from intermediate stations.

| | |
|---|---|
| BIRKENHEAD, CHESTER SHREWSBURY, WOLVERHAMPTON BIRMINGHAM, LEAMINGTON SPA BANBURY, OXFORD *and* BRIGHTON, HASTINGS, RAMSGATE MARGATE, FOLKESTONE, DOVER & DEAL | BIRKENHEAD, CHESTER MANCHESTER, SHREWSBURY WOLVERHAMPTON BIRMINGHAM, LEAMINGTON SPA, BANBURY, OXFORD *and* SOUTHAMPTON, PORTSMOUTH & BOURNEMOUTH |

## RESTAURANT CAR TRAINS
### also
CARDIFF, NEWPORT, BRISTOL (Stapleton Road), BATH and WORTHING, HOVE & BRIGHTON

*For full particulars see the Company's Official Time Tables and Notices.*

A great many of the services to Portsmouth and Bournemouth made use of the GWR routes available. The following show long distance trains with definite Southern associations. Here, 30736 races through Tilehurst, north-west of Reading, with the 11.55 Wolverhampton-Bournemouth, 17 September 1955.
*R.C. Riley*

'King Arthur' No 30782 *Sir Brian* takes the 10.23 am York-Bournemouth West out of Oxford on 29 September 1956.
*R.C. Riley*

The rebuilt Banbury station sees 'Hall' Class 4-6-0 No 6934 *Beachamwell Hall* leave with the 3.40 pm Portsmouth-Wolverhampton Low Level on 6 August 1960.
*M. Mensing*

'Modified Hall' No 7911 *Lady Margaret Hall* races through Harbury Cutting, south of Leamington Spa with the 9.20 am Birkenhead-Bournemouth on 13 September, 1956. The Southern Maunsell coaching stock at the front of the train looks to have seen better days.
*M. Mensing*

Yet another GWR 'Hall', this time No 5921 *Bingley Hall* makes the summit of Hatton Bank with the 3.40 pm Portsmouth Harbour-Wolverhampton Low Level on 18 July 1959. Again, a combination of GWR motive power and Southern stock.
*M. Mensing*

Double-heading a really mixed set of stock 4300 Class 2-6-0 No 5381 pilots standard Class 5 4-6-0 No 73035 through Acock's Green and South Yardley on the GWR's southern outskirts of Birmingham. The train is the 8.50 am Portsmouth Harbour-Birmingham Snow Hill working. 16 August 1958.
*M. Mensing*

Having stepped out of a Meccano or Hornby Dublo advertisement, a boy watches in the 9.30 am Bournemouth West-Birkenhead at Birmingham Snow Hill, Saturday 4 July 1959. The locomotive is 'Hall' No 4925 *Eynsham Hall*; the time is 3.05pm.
*M. Mensing*

Birmingham Moor Street was also used to take the pressure off Snow Hill on Summer Saturdays. Here 'Castle' No 5065 *Newport Castle* arrives with the 1.11 pm departure from Portsmouth Harbour 2 July 1960.
*M. Mensing*

A long way from the 'Sunny South Coast' but still with some considerable distance to cover, the fireman takes the opportunity to reorganise his coal and take on water at Wolverhampton Low Level – 4 July 1959. No 4925 *Eynsham Hall* offers up some smoke effects as it replenishes with the 9.30 am Bournemouth West-Birkenhead.     *M. Mensing*

Running through the Shropshire countryside, 'Hall' No 4902 *Aldenham Hall* takes the 9.30 Bournemouth-Birkenhead towards Wellington on 12 September 1959.     *M. Mensing*

Back in the West Country, 'Modified Hall' No 7925, *Westol Hall* leaves Trowbridge in Wiltshire with the 10.30 am Cardiff-Portsmouth and Southsea service on 4 May 1963.
*M. Mensing*

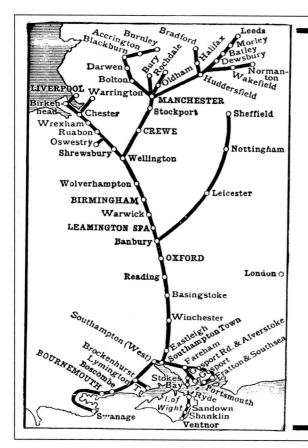

The ex Great Central Railway played a useful role in developing traffic between the North East, East Midlands and the South Coast via Banbury, linking in with the GWR.
In this first of three views is a decided terminal atmosphere. The daily Bournemouth-York is seen here passing an increasingly derelict Charwelton, south of Rugby. Demolition prevails as what is now a Class 47 diesel-electric, then numbered D1769, heads north on a railway doomed to never fulfil its obvious potential.

*M. Mensing*

An earlier more familiar scene, further north, sees Class B1 4-6-0 No 61369 working the York-Bournemouth, north of Lutterworth on the G.C. main line. 12 September 1956.

*M. Mensing*

Another B1 this time No 61078 works northward with the 11.16 am Bournemouth-Newcastle near Pilsley in the Chesterfield district. 29 September 1959. *M. Mensing*

The main LMS route to the South Coast from the Midlands and North-West relied heavily on the ex Midland line southward from Birmingham to Bath thence by the S & D to Bournemouth. The route southward through Birmingham New Street towards Bristol also carried substantial holiday traffic to the West Country. At New Street in June 1957, the Sheffield-Bournemouth coach is attached to the southbound *Pines Express* by Stanier 5 No 44839. *M. Mensing*

# NORTH AND MIDLANDS TO THE SOUTH AND SOUTH-EAST OF ENGLAND.
## VIA BANBURY AND OXFORD.

**UP**      **WEEK DAYS.**      **SUNDAYS.**

| Station | a.m. | a.m. | p.m. | p.m. | a.m. | p.m. | a.m. | | | | | a.m. | |
|---|---|---|---|---|---|---|---|---|---|---|---|---|---|
| ABERDEEN ....................dep | | | 5 15 | | | | 8 45 | | | | | | |
| Dundee (Tay Bridge) ............ " | | | 7 10 | | | | 10 49 | | | | | | |
| St. Andrews ................ " | | | 7 13 | | | | 10 15 | | | | | | |
| Perth ........................ " | | | 7 50 | | | | 12 40 p.m | | | | | | |
| GLASGOW (Queen Street) ... " | | | 7 55 | | | | 1 0 | | | | | | |
| EDINBURGH .............. " | | | 10 0 | | | | 2 25 | | | | | | |
| Berwick ...................... " | | | 8 29 | | 7 5 | | 4 21 | | | | | | |
| NEWCASTLE ............... " | | | 10 10 | a.m. | 9 5 | | 7 15 | | | | | | |
| Sunderland ................ " | | | 9 25 | p.m. | 9 31 | | 6 10 | | | | | | |
| Durham ...................... " | | | 11 4 | | 10 33 | | 7 43 | | | | | | |
| Darlington .................. " | | | 10 19 | a.m. | 11 10 | | 8 23 | | | | | | |
| West Hartlepool ............ " | | | 8 55 | p.m. | 9 35 | | 6 50 | | | | | | |
| Middlesbro' .................. " | | | 10 45 | | 9 58 | | 7 30 | | | | | | |
| STOCKTON .................. " | | | 9 24 | | 10 8 | | 7 25 | | | | | | |
| Thirsk ........................ " | | | 9 15 | | 7 22 | | 9 13 | | | | | | |
| Scarborough ................ " | | | | | 10 33 | | 8 5 | | | | | | |
| Harrogate (via York) ........ " | | | a.m. | | 11 0 | | 7 15 | | | | | | |
| YORK ........................ " | | | 8 17 | | 12 19 | | 10 0 | | | | | | |
| LIVERPOOL (Central) ........dep | | | 8 10 | | 12 30 | 2 5 | 6 20 | | | | | | |
| Southport (Lord Street) ...... " | | | 7 15 | | 9 50 | 1 12 | 5 20 | | | | | | |
| Warrington (Central) ........ " | | | 8 39 | | 12 50 | 2 31 | 6 49 | | | | | | |
| Wigan ........................ " | | | 6 40 | | 9 50 | 2 10 | 4 45 | | | | | | |
| St. Helens .................... " | | | | | 10 0 | 2 15 | 5 42 | | | | | | |
| Stockport (Tiviot Dale) ...... " | | | | | 10 30 | 3 04 | 6 32 | | | | | | |
| MANCHESTER {Central / London Rd} " | | | 9 25 | | 3 20 | | 7 20 | | | | | 6 50 | |
| | | | 10 0 | | 2 15 | 3 40 | 6 30 | | | | | | |
| Fallowfield for Withington and Didsbury " | | | 9 35 | | | | | | | | | | |
| Oldham (Clegg Street) ...... " | | | 9 12 | | 2 2 | | 7 17 | | | | | | |
| Stalybridge .................. " | | | 9 31 | | 2 10 | | 6 45 | | | | | | |
| Guide Bridge ................ " | | | 10 11 | | 2 26 | 3 41 | 7 42 | | | | | 7 10 | |
| BRADFORD (Exchange) ......dep | | | 10 0 | | 35 | | 6 25 | | | | | | |
| HALIFAX ...................... " | | | 9 53 | | 20 | | 6 50 | | | | | | |
| HUDDERSFIELD ............ " | | | 10 33 | | 2 13 | | 7 18 | | | | | 7 40 | |
| Barnsley (Court House)........dep | | | 8 20 | | 12 18 | 4 30 | 6 31 | | | | | 6 30 | |
| Penistone .................... " | | | 10 50 | | 3 7 | | 8 23 | | | | | 8 32 | |
| Hull {Corporation Pier / Paragon} " | | | 7 55 | | 11 45 | | 6 35 | | | | | | |
| Grimsby Docks .............. " | | | 8 53 | | 11 38 | 12 | 5 55 | | | | | | |
| Grimsby Town .............. " | | | | | 1 33 | | 6 1 | | | | | | |
| Gainsborough .............. " | | | 9 50 | | 2 20 | | 6 46 | | | | | | |
| Lincoln ...................... " | | | 9 20 | | 1 18 | 2 30 | 6 30 | | | | | | |
| Retford ...................... " | | | 10 13 | | 1 50 | 3 50 | 7 28 | | | | | | |
| Worksop ...................... " | | | 9 38 | | 2 57 | 3 8 | 7 12 | | | | | | |
| Doncaster .................... " | | | 9 50 | | 2 30 | 4 28 | 8 15 | | | | | | |
| ROTHERHAM AND MASBORO' ... " | | | 10 21 | | 11 0 | | 11 0 | | | | | | |
| SHEFFIELD (Victoria) ........dep | | 5 5 | 11 21 | | 1 26 | 4 55 | 9 48 | | | | | 9 18 | |
| CHESTERFIELD (Central) ...... " | | 6 0 | | | 3 31 | | 7 50 | | | | | | |
| MANSFIELD (G.C.) ............ " | | | 11 23 | | 3 18 | | 10 10 | | | | | | |
| NOTTINGHAM (Victoria) ... " | 5 18 | 7 57 | 12 14 | | 3 15 | 5 59 | 12 35 | 12 a.m. | | | | 10 15 | |
| LOUGHBORO' .................. " | 5 45 | 8 27 | 12 52 | | | | 10 42 | 10 22 p.m. | | | | | |
| LEICESTER (Central) ........ " | 6 12 | 8 53 | 1 10 | | 3 57 | 6 36 | 1 18 | 1 18 a.m. | | | | 10 49 | |
| RUGBY (Central) ............ " | 6 51 | 9 38 | 1 49 | | 5 26 | 7 23 | 1 46 | 1 56 | | | | 11 16 | |
| Woodford and Hinton {arr / dep} | 7 17 | 10 2 | 2 16 p.m. | | 0 16 | 7 3 | | | | | | | |
| | 7 15 | 10 25 | 2 27 | 1 15 | | 7 35 | | | | | | | |
| Eydon Road Halt .............. " | 7 52 | 10 32 | 2 35 | 4 22 | | 7 43 | | | | | | | |
| Chalcombe Road Halt ........ " | 8 0 | 10 11 | 2 41 | 4 37 | | 7 50 | | | | | | | |
| BANBURY {arr / dep} | 8 7 | 10 48 | 2 52 | 4 37 | 7 6 | 7 50 | 2 23 | 2 23 | | | 11 47 | | |
| | 8 37 | 11 7 | 3 0 | | 7 9 | | 2 45 | 2 45 | | | 11 50 | | |
| OXFORD {arr / dep} | 9 5 | 12 0 | 3 30 | 4 36 | | | 3 15 | 3 15 | | | 12 18 | | |
| | 9 35 | 12 25 | 4 30 | 5 43 | | | 7 5 | 7 30 | | | 12 25 | | |
| Didcot ....................arr | 10 2 | 12 52 | 5 0 | 5 5 | 9 20 | | 7 30 | 7 55 | | | 12 40 | | |
| Reading (G.W. Rly.) .......... " | 10 57 | 1 3 | 5 5 | 6 10 | 9 35 | | 8 32 | 8 41 | | | 1 47 | | |
| Reading (S.E. & C. Rly.) ......arr | 11 15 | 1 50 | 6 25 | 8 15 | 10 0 | | | | | | 4 10 | | |
| Aldershot Town ............ " | 12 51 | 2 58 | 7 35 | 9 0 1 | 10 30 | | | | | | 6 6 | | |
| Guildford .................... " | 12 58 | 3 0 | 7 37 | 9 21 | 10 29 | | | | | | 6 21 | | |
| Redhill ...................... " | 1 55 | 4 4 | 8 13 | 10 33 | 11 35 | | | | | | 6 31 | | |
| Brighton .................... " | 4 13 | 5 10 | 11 1 | | 1 47 | | | | | | 9 13 | | |
| Worthing .................... " | 4 50 | 5 50 | 11 45 | | 2 6 | | | | | | 9 9 | | |
| Newhaven .................... " | 4 50 | 6 33 | | | 2 9 | | | | | | 9 6 | | |
| Eastbourne .................. " | 5 7 | 7 37 | 12 17 | | 2 53 | | | | | | 9 0 | | |
| Tunbridge Wells ............ " | 3 15 | 6 18 | | | 3 15 | | | | | | 10 52 | | |
| Hastings .................... " | 4 27 | 8 0 5 | | | 4 5 | | | | | | 10 0 | | |
| Deal .......................... " | 7 21 | 9 5 | 2 1 | | 3 15 | | | | | | 10 0 | | |
| Canterbury (West) .......... " | 6 31 | 8 15 | 1 10 | | 3 30 | | | | | | 10 51 | | |
| Ramsgate (Town) ............ " | 7 38 | 9 0 | | | 4 5 | | | | | | 11 8 | | |
| Margate (Sands) ............ " | 7 10 | 9 11 | | | 4 15 | | | | | | 9 50 | | |
| Folkestone (Central) ........ " | 5 12 | 8 10 | 12 50 | | 3 25 | | | | | | 11 5 | | |
| Dover (Harbour) ............ " | 7 55 | 9 30 | 2 28 | | 4 40 | | | | | | 11 30 | | |
| Newbury ....................arr | 11 30 | 10 31 | 6 6 | 7 5 15 | 8 25 | | | | | | 7 14 | | |
| Lambourn .................... " | | 5 8 | 7 17 | | 9 51 | | | | | | | | |
| Winchester (Cheesehill) ...... " | 12 57 | 5 30 | 7 53 | | 9 40 | | | | | | | | |
| Eastleigh (via Newbury) ...... " | 1 16 | 5 51 | 8 11 | | 10 0 | | | | | | | | |
| BASINGSTOKE {arr / dep} | 12 35 | 2 25 | 5 57 | 7 30 | 10 48 | 9 21 | | | | | 7 5 | | |
| | 12 54 | 4 32 | 5 59 | 7 35 | | 9 35 | 11 50 | | | | 7 29 | | |
| WINCHESTER (L. & S.W.) ...arr | 1 25 | 5 2 | 6 47 | 8 24 | 30 | 10 3 | 12 12 | | | | 8 4 | | |
| Eastleigh (via Basingstoke) ... " | 1 40 | 5 16 | 7 8 | | | 10 18 | 12 24 | | | | 8 18 | | |
| Gosport ...................... " | | | | | | | | | | | | | |
| PORTSMOUTH (Town) ...... " | 2 37 | 6 45 | 8 49 | 9 47 | 2 11 | 11 43 | 1 9 | | | | 10 18 | | |
| SOUTHAMPTON {Tn. for Dks. / West} " | 1 27 | 5 34 | 7 26 | 9 55 | | 10 38 | 1 4 | | | | 10 42 | | |
| | 1 50 | 5 46 | | | | 10 56 | 1 19 | | | | 5 | | |
| Cowes (Boat) ................ " | 3 25 | 6 55 | | | | 12 33 | 3 25 | | | | | | |
| Newport {I.W.C. Rly.} " | 3 55 | | | | | 12 57 | 3 55 | | | | | | |
| Sandown " | 5 18 | | | | | 1 18 | 5 | | | | | | |
| Ventnor Town " | 4 30 | | | | | 1 47 | 4 30 | | | | | | |
| Freshwater (F. Y. & N. Rly.) ... " | 5 F 2 | | | | | | | | | | | | |
| Lyndhurst Road ............ " | 2 18 | 7 15 | | 9 20 | | 11 17 | 1 39 | | | | 9 33 | | |
| Brockenhurst ................ " | 3 4 | 6 13 | | 9 19 | 12 50 | 11 33 | 1 50 | | | | 9 41 | | |
| Lymington .................... " | 2 50 | | | | | 11 48 | 1 59 | | | | | | |
| {Yarmouth I. of W. (Boat) / Newport I.of W.(F.Y. & N.R)} " | 3 30 | | | | | 1 30 | | | | | | | |
| | 6 17 | | | | | 2 42 | | | | | | | |
| Christchurch ................ " | 3 35 | 6 50 | | 9 40 | 1 35 | 11 21 | 1 55 | | | | 9 49 | | |
| Boscombe .................... " | 3 41 | 6 50 | | 9 48 | | 11 30 | 2 45 | | | | 9 55 | | |
| BOURNEMOUTH {Cen. / W.} " | 3 49 | 7 4 | | 9 52 | 1 46 | 11 43 | 2 49 | | | | 10 1 | | |
| | 5 0 | 7 25 | | | | | | | | | | 10 22 | |

# HAMPSHIRE'S RAILWAY CONNECTIONS

Through carriages from: SHEFFIELD, NOTTINGHAM, LEICESTER, RUGBY, WOLVERHAMPTON, BIRMINGHAM, LEAMINGTON, BANBURY, OXFORD. AND READING to PORTSMOUTH, SOUTHAMPTON, BROCKENHURST, NEW MILTON & BOURNEMOUTH.
Also from: NEWCASTLE, YORK, BRADFORD, BIRKENHEAD, CHESTER, SHREWSBURY to SOUTHAMPTON, BROCKENHURST, NEW MILTON & BOURNEMOUTH.

Through carriages from: BRADFORD, LEEDS, SHEFFIELD, MANCHESTER, LIVERPOOL, STOCKPORT, CREWE, BIRMINGHAM, CHELTENHAM & BATH to BOURNEMOUTH WEST.

Through carriages from: CARDIFF, NEWPORT, BRISTOL, BATH & WESTBURY TO SOUTHAMPTON, AND PORTSMOUTH (VIA ROMSEY). ALSO TO BOURNEMOUTH AND NEW MILTON (VIA WIMBORNE AND POOLE).

LONDON
WATERLOO     VICTORIA
SURBITON     SUTTON
WOKING
GUILDFORD     DORKING NORTH
BASINGSTOKE     HORSHAM
WINCHESTER
HASLEMERE
TEMPLECOMBE     SALISBURY
MAIN LINE FROM EXETER CENTRAL     ROMSEY
EASTLEIGH
PETERSFIELD     ARUNDEL
FROM BRIGHTON
WIMBORNE     SOUTHAMPTON     HAVANT     CHICHESTER
BROCKENHURST     FAREHAM
BROADSTONE     BOAT FROM ROYAL PIER
POOLE     HAYLING ISLAND
NEW MILTON     FRATTON
CHRISTCHURCH     LYMINGTON Pier     PORTSMOUTH & SOUTHSEA
POKESDOWN     PORTSMOUTH HARBOUR
BOSCOMBE     CAR FERRY
BOURNEMOUTH CENTRAL     FISHBOURNE
PASSENGER & CAR FERRY →     COWES     RYDE Pier
BOURNEMOUTH WEST     RYDE Esplanade
YARMOUTH
NEWPORT     SANDOWN
Isle of Wight     SHANKLIN
VENTNOR

■■■■■■■■■■ STEAMER CONNECTION

*Holiday Haunts, 1960*

# Chapter Five
# POST WAR PERSPECTIVE: CONTINUITY AND CHANGE

Nationalisation in 1948 allocated the Somerset and Dorset, the Reading-Basingstoke and the Westbury-Salisbury lines, together with the Channel Islands shipping services at Weymouth, to the Southern Region. Later readjustments, giving the Western Region increased and, eventually, complete control over the S and D, played no small part in its demise. Deep into austerity, mid-forties Britain lacked the stylish confidence of the pre-war years, but there was a gradual return to former standards. Until the mid to late sixties, there was limited competition from foreign holiday travel and for two decades, at least, the English seaside resorts, served by the railways, enjoyed continued popularity and prosperity, peaking in the mid-fifties. Southern Railway motive power was given a decided boost through the work of Oliver Bulleid, Chief Mechanical Engineer, 1937-1949. His "Merchant Navy" pacifics, beginning with "Channel Packet" in March 1941 and followed by the later and lighter version, the "West Country/Battle of Britain" class of the summer of 1945 characterised many post-war express trains. "Standard" classes were also adopted in the '50s.

Isle of Wight services benefited from the introduction of three modern oil-burning ferries for the Portsmouth-Ryde crossing. *Southsea* and *Brading* entered service in 1948 with *Shanklin* following in 1951. Records for the early fifties show that almost four million passengers were carried to the Island during the year, principally to the coastal resorts of Ryde, Sandown, Shanklin and Ventnor. Seat reservation was essential, as stressed by British Railways timetables, and there were the inevitable queues that characterised summer seasons on the Island.

Despite this, there were line closures; four sections over a four-year period during the fifties. The first to succumb was the Merstone-Ventnor West line, the last to be opened, the final section here being as late as June 1900. Services ceased on 13 September 1952, giving the line a life of just over half a century. One year later, the Newport, Yarmouth and Freshwater line followed, services ending on 21 September 1953. That same day also marked the closure of the Bembridge branch from Brading. It was a further 5½ years to the next closure, this being the Newport-Sandown line, on 6 February 1956. Thus, the Isle of Wight entered the sixties with only two lines – the original Isle of Wight Railway from Ryde to Ventnor dating from 1864, and the Isle of Wight Central line from Ryde to Newport and Cowes, the Newport-Cowes section being the Island's first project, opened in June 1862.

Further closures followed in 1966 when the Ryde-Cowes route shut down on 21 February that year. Ventnor, likewise, was not to see another summer season in terms of railway operations. The resort lost its link with Shanklin and Ryde when the four-mile section from Shanklin through Wroxhall to Ventnor was closed on 18 April. Shanklin was now the terminus, the Island's railway system having been reduced from 55½ miles to just 8 miles, in less than 15 years. Another obvious watershed for the Island's railway history came on the last day of 1966, making this a year of special significance. New Year's Eve marked the final day of steam working. Seven locomotives were in steam,

bringing a little more than a century of experience to an end. The line was then closed for engineering purposes, namely, the installation of electrified working, using refurbished London Transport Underground stock dating back to pre-war days.

A very different Isle of Wight Railway reopened on 20 March 1967. Whilst the Ryde-Shanklin service took on somewhat ironic trappings, a confused identity of would-be modern working, steam refused to die. Today, one can choose the electric line to Shanklin, or the Isle of Wight Steam Railway, operating in season, over the former Isle of Wight Central Railway route, from Smallbrook westward to Wootton. Haven Street is, again, a passing place, as it became in 1926 under the Southern Railway. In their own way, the Isle of Wight Railway and the Isle of Wight Central Railway have sustained a competitive character, albeit, modified and re-defined according to the developments of the late twentieth century. Electric services to Shanklin and the active presence of the preservationists at Haven Street reflect the important elements of continuity and change in the Island's overall experience.

In a break, perhaps pause, from austerity, 'The Festival of Britain' was something of a celebration in 1951. As part of the event and atmosphere, British Railway's Southern Region marked the occasion with the introduction of a new named express, *The Royal Wessex*, running between Waterloo and Bournemouth, Swanage and Weymouth. Commencing on 3 May 1951 the 'up' train departed Bournemouth Central at 8.40 am, arriving Waterloo at 10.54 am. The return working departed Waterloo at 4.35 pm, arriving Bournemouth Central at 7.03 pm (Swanage 8.00 pm/Weymouth 8.03 pm). Shorn of its two hour non-stop timing, *The Royal Wessex* was something of a revived *Bournemouth Limited*. The new train was hauled on its first day by the Southern Railway's West County Light Pacifics – Bulleid 4-6-2s class of 1945 vintage, in this case, the initial 'down' train with No 34008 *Padstow*, and the morning 'up' working with No 34105 *Swanage*. British Railways standard coaching stock was provided for the new services, although this changed to Bulleid, Southern Railway sets from 1962.

The summer season of 1962 has particular significance for holiday traffic to and from Bournemouth. This was the last season for through trains over the Somerset and Dorset route, and, duly, on 8 September that year, 9F class 2-10-0 No 92220, *Evening Star* headed the last *Pines Express*, the S & D's most famous train. Four 9F locomotives had been assigned to Bath for duties on the Somerset and Dorset during the season of 1960. Evening Star made the appropriate choice for the final working. With the end of the 1962 season *The Pines Express* and all former through workings to Bournemouth West were re-routed via Banbury, Oxford and Basingstoke. The Somerset and Dorset route itself only survived for another three summers, albeit, on a local traffic basis, the entire line closing on 6 March 1966. Another significant cross-country trunk route, directly associated with through traffic to the South Coast also closed in 1966. From 5 September that year, the ex Great Central main line north of Aylesbury, to

Locomotive changes at New Street for *The Pines Express*. The northbound train has been brought to Birmingham by D121 diesel electric, but steam takes over for the final section to Manchester in the shape of 'Royal Scot' 4-6-0 No 46149, *The Middlesex Regiment* 24 March 1962. *M. Mensing*

Heading north through the Gloucestershire countryside near Coaley, Stanier Class 5 No 44658 makes good progress with the 12.20 pm Bournemouth West-Nottingham Midland on Saturday 7 July 1962. *M. Mensing*

Not the most important but probably best known route to Bournemouth was that of the Somerset and Dorset. Abounding in steep inclines, harsh curvatures and single-line section it was never easy to work. The following views show the S & D at work on Summer Saturdays.
Set back into the sidings at Wellow 7F 2-8-0 No 53807 makes way for the 'up' *Pines Express* headed by Standard Class 5 No 73049. 6 July 1959. *R.C. Riley*

7F 2-8-0 No 53806 climbs the 1 in 50s on each side of Midsomer Norton, where the gradient eases through the station itself. The train is the southbound 7.32 am Nottingham-Bournemouth West; the date, 11 August 1960. So there are two further seasons of long-distance traffic to follow. *R.C. Riley*

Another 7F runs downhill form Windsor Hill Tunnel with the same train, the 7.32 Nottingham-Bournemouth West on 28 July 1962. The locomotive was No 53808.
*R.C. Riley*

Rugby, was closed. The link through Banbury was no more and the remnant of the *GCR*, between Nottingham and Rugby, survived for a further three years, closing on 3 May 1969.

Given the significance of the considerable, if inevitable, closure to through holiday traffic over the S and D in 1962 this particular season would seem to make a fitting example by way of the later post-war services, prior to their nationalisation, or, indeed, extinction thereafter. 1962 marked the end of an era in more ways than one.

The full Summer Saturday service timetable, 1962, for long distance travel is given here – Bournemouth West and Bournemouth Central:

## BOURNEMOUTH WEST: DEPARTURES, S AND D
7.12 am – Templecombe arr 8.05 am
8.40 am – Derby arr 3.06 pm
8.48 am – Templecombe arr 10.15 am
9.25 am – Liverpool/Manchester Piccadilly arr 4.49/5.01 pm
9.45 am – *The Pines Express* Manchester Piccadilly arr 5.40 pm
10.05 am – Bradford arr 7.54 pm
10.32 am – Manchester Victoria arr 6.47 pm
11.12 am – Sheffield Midland arr 6.25 pm
12.20 pm – Nottingham Midland arr 7.41 pm
1.08 pm – Bristol Temple Meads arr 5.17 pm
3.40 pm – Bristol Temple Meads arr 7.44 pm
5.30 pm – Templecombe arr 7.01 pm
6.48 pm – Templecombe arr 8.11 pm
10.00 pm – Templecombe arr 11.17 pm

## BOURNEMOUTH WEST: ARRIVALS S AND D
5.00 am – Derby dep 11.10 pm F.O.
6.01 am – Bradford dep 8.25 am 27 July – 24 Aug.
6.01 am – Sheffield Midland dep 10.20 pm 29 June – 20 July, from 31 Aug
6.44 am – Manchester Piccadilly dep 10.28 pm
9.05 am – Templecombe dep 7.35 am
10.47 am – Bristol Temple Meads dep 5.58 am
12.54 pm – Bristol Temple Meads dep 9.03 am
1.57 pm – Templecombe dep 12.23 pm
2.55 pm – Birmingham New St dep 9.08 am
3.10 pm – Nottingham Midland dep 7.32 am
5.35 pm – Bradford dep 7.45 am
6.08 pm – *The Pines Express* Manchester Piccadilly dep 10.25 am
6.43 pm – Templecombe dep 5.12 p,
7.05 pm – Liverpool Lime St dep 10.30/Manchester Piccadilly dep 10.55 am
10.31 pm – Bristol dep 6.08 pm

## BOURNEMOUTH CENTRAL: DEPARTURES
5.47 am – Eastleigh arr 7.17 am
6.22 am – Waterloo arr 10.49 am
6.50 am – Brockenhurst arr 7.27 am
7.30 am – Waterloo arr 10.00 am dep West 7.20 am
7.35 am – Southampton Terminus arr 8.55 dep West 7.25 am
8.05 am – Newcastle Central arr 6.49 pm
8.23 am – Waterloo arr 11.58 dep West 8.12 am
8.40 am – *The Royal Wessex* Waterloo arr 10.51 am
8.45 am – Waterloo arr 11.58 dep West 8.35 am
9.00 am – Cardiff arr 1.30 pm
9.13 am – Swansea arr 3.53 pm dep New Milton 8.48 am

9.20 am – Waterloo arr 11.34 am
9.30 am – Wolverhampton Low Level arr 2.30 dep West 0.20 am
9.40 am – Birkenhead arr 6.03 pm
10.00 am – Waterloo arr 12.26 pm
10.20 am – Waterloo arr 12.39 pm
10.30 am – Waterloo arr 12.50 pm
10.42 am – Bradford arr 7.42 pm dep Poole 10.25 am
10.50 am – Waterloo arr 1.42 pm Dep West 10.40 am
11.00 am – Sheffield Victoria arr 7.00 pm
11.10 am – Waterloo arr 2. 11 pm dep West 11.00 am
11.26 am – Newcastle arr 9.44 pm dep West 11.16 am
11.36 am – Eastleigh arr 1.05 pm
12.20 pm – Waterloo arr 2.40 pm dep West 12.10 pm
12.40 pm – Waterloo arr 2.50 pm
1.16 pm – Waterloo arr 4.14 pm dep West 1.05 pm
1.48 pm – Waterloo arr 4.04 pm
1.55 pm – Brighton arr 4.54 pm dep West 1.45 pm
2.14 pm – Waterloo arr 4.42 pm
2.30 pm – Waterloo arr 4.44 pm dep West 2.20 pm
2.38 pm – Waterloo arr 4.50 pm
3.16 pm – Waterloo arr 6.32 pm dep West 3.05 pm
3.35 pm – Eastleigh arr 5.00 pm
4.25 pm – Waterloo arr 6.58 pm dep West 4.15 pm
4.30 pm – Bournemouth Belle – Waterloo arr 6.46 pm
4.33 pm – Eastleigh arr 5.54 pm
5.16 pm – Waterloo arr 8.25 pm
5.35 pm – Eastleigh arr 6.37 pm
6.26 pm – Waterloo arr 8.41 pm dep West 6.16 pm
6.46 pm – Waterloo arr 10.46 dep West 6.36 pm
7.32 pm – Eastleigh arr 8.53 pm
7.50 pm – Waterloo arr 10.56 pm
9.20 pm – Reading arr 12.18 am
10.48 pm – Southampton Central arr 11.43 pm
11.36 pm – Waterloo arr 3.48 am

## BOURNEMOUTH CENTRAL: ARRIVALS
6.05 am – Waterloo dep 2.55 am
7.35 am – Eastleigh dep 6.03 am
8.16 am – Newcastle dep 9.43 pm
8.32 am – Brockenhurst dep 7.56 pm arr West 8.44 pm
8.53 am – Waterloo dep 5.40 am
9.24 am – Eastleigh dep 7.50 am
9.31 am – Waterloo dep 7.20 am
10.07 am – Eastleigh dep 8.40 am
10.24 am – Waterloo dep 8.22 am
10.56 am – Waterloo dep 8.30 am
11.18 am – Basingstoke dep 9.30 am
11.52 am – Southampton dep 10.30 am
11.58 am – Waterloo dep 9.24 am
12.09 pm – Brighton dep 9.40 am arr 12.23 West
12.19 pm – Waterloo dep 9.35 am arr 12.30 West
12.27 pm – Wimbledon dep 9.25 am
12.38 pm – Waterloo dep 10.05 am
12.46 pm – Waterloo dep 10.30 am
1.18 pm – Eastleigh dep 11.53 am
1.35 pm – Waterloo dep 11.05 am arr 1.47 West
1.54 pm – Waterloo dep 11.22 am
2.10 pm – Eastleigh dep 12.50 pm
2.20 pm – Cardiff dep 9.32 pm
2.23 pm – Waterloo dep 11.30 am
2.40 pm – Bournemouth Belle dep Waterloo 12.30 arr 2.52 West
2.51 pm – Waterloo dep 12.35 pm
3.33 pm – Eastleigh dep 2.05 pm arr 3.45 pm West

West Country Pacifics, both unrebuilt examples, cross at Evercreech Junction on 6 July 1959. *Combe Martin* 34043 heads the 'down' *Pines Express* whilst No 34044, *Woolacombe* is in charge of an empty stock working.                  *R.C. Riley*

The final S & D example here sees 9F 2-10-0 No 92001 working twelve coaches of the 'up' *Pines Express* through Sturminster Newton on 4 July 1961.
*R.C. Riley*

| | |
|---|---|
| 3.50 pm | – Waterloo dep 1.22 pm |
| 3.56 pm | – Swansea dep 9.55 am arr Brockenhurst 4.30 pm |
| 4.00 pm | – Sheffield Victoria dep 8.55 am |
| 4.20 pm | – Waterloo dep 1.30 pm |
| 4.34 pm | – Waterloo dep 2.22 pm arr 4.55 pm West |
| 4.50 pm | – Waterloo dep 2.30 pm |
| 5.23 pm | – Southampton Terminus dep 4.05 pm |
| 5.31 pm | – Birkenhead Woodside dep 9.30 am |
| 5.40 pm | – Waterloo dep 3.20 arr 5.57 West |
| 6.26 pm | – Waterloo dep 3.30 arr 6.40 West |
| 6.40 pm | – Bradford Exchange dep 10.00 am arr Poole 6.54 pm |
| 6.57 pm | – *Royal Wessex* Waterloo dep 4.35 arr 7.13 West |
| 7.16 pm | – Newcastle Central dep 8.30 am arr 7.28 West |
| 7.27 pm | – Southampton Term dep 6.10 p, |
| 8.17 pm | – Waterloo dep 5.30 arr 8.29 West |
| 8.37 pm | – Waterloo dep 6.30 pm |
| 9.31 pm | – Southampton Central dep 8.05 pm |

10.13 pm – Waterloo dep 7.30 arr 10.27 West
10.44 pm – Through coaches from 7.30 dep Waterloo,
           stopping service from Southampton
           Central
12.09 am – Waterloo dep 9.30 pm arr 12.23 Poole
2.02 am  – Waterloo dep 11.35 pm
2.11 am  – Waterloo dep 10.35 pm via Southampton
           Terminus

## PORTSMOUTH AND SOUTHSEA (PS) AND PORTSMOUTH HARBOUR (PH)

ARRIVALS – Cross-Country Services, excluding Waterloo and local regional traffic, e.g. Salisbury, Andover, Southampton and the Mid-Sussex and Brighton lines – a substantial service. The achievement of course, was made all the more impressive when one includes the 47 express trains in each direction between Waterloo and Portsmouth on Summer Saturdays, this being the timetable that year at its fullest extent. Even so, this was something of a reduction on the timetable of the mid-fifties. In 1955 there were 50 such trains in each direction, 40 of them offering Buffet and Restaurant Car services.

P H 4.13 am   – Nottingham Victoria dep 10.55 pm
                13 July – 25 Aug
P H 4.23 am   – Sheffield Victoria dep 9.55 pm
P H 10.12 am  – Bristol dep 8.17 am
P S 10.50 am  – Reading dep 9.53 am
P H 12.10 pm  – Bristol dep 8.17 am
P H 1.01 pm   – Birmingham Moor St dep 8.40 am
P H 1.36 pm   – Wolverhampton Low Level
                dep 8.40 am
P S 1.36 pm   – Cardiff dep 9.06 am
P H 2.01 pm   – Bristol dep 10.50 am
P H 2.23 pm   – Birmingham Snow Hill dep 9.50 am
P S 2.36 pm   – Cardiff dep 10.05 am
P S 3.04 pm   – Cardiff 10.40 am
P S 3.35 pm   – Reading dep 1.53 pm
P S 3.49 pm   – Plymouth dep 10.02 am
P H 5.16 pm   – Cardiff dep 12.50 pm
P S 6.43 pm   – Reading dep 5.00 pm
P S 8.14 pm   – Bristol dep 5.00 pm
P S 9.05 pm   – Cardiff dep 4.25 pm
P S 10.52 pm  – Bristol dep 7.25 pm

Portsmouth and Southsea PS and Portsmouth
Harbour PH

DEPARTURES
P S 8.30 am   – Bristol arr 12.02 pm
P S 9.03 am   – Plymouth arr 2.53 pm
P H 9.11 am   – Wolverhampton Low Level 1.51 pm
P H 9.27 am   – Cardiff arr 2.22 pm
P S 10.34 am  – Cardiff arr 3.27 pm
P H 11.37 am  – Cardiff arr 4.2 pm
P S 12.15 pm  – Ilfracombe arr 6.15, Torrington
                arr 6.11 pm
P H 1.11 pm   – Birmingham Moor St arr 5.21 pm
P H 1.28 pm   – Birmingham Snow Hill arr 5.53 pm
P S 2.43 pm   – Bristol arr 6.15 pm
P H 3.02 pm   – Nottingham Victoria arr 7.55 pm
P S 3.45 pm   – Reading arr 5.47 pm
P H 3.50 pm   – Wolverhampton Low Level
                arr 8.42 pm
P H 3.57 pm   – Cardiff arr 8.45 pm
P H 4.40 pm   – Sheffield Victoria arr 11.10 pm
P S 5.45 pm   – Cardiff arr 10.33 pm
P S 8.54 pm   – Reading arr 10.44 pm

Such an extensive and varied timetable as this, on the eve of the Beeching Report, testifies to the sustained popularity and success of the Portsmouth, Isle of Wight and Bournemouth areas as holiday locations. They exemplified the Southern's 'Sunny South Coast', and whilst the 1962 timetable reflected a certain reduction in the provision of long distance workings as on the Somerset and Dorset, for example, since the mid fifties, the overall structure of services remained intact.

Sunshine imagery, however, was not uppermost in railway terms in the years that followed. Closures and cuts came to bear from 1962 itself. As mentioned, the closure of the Somerset and Dorset to all through traffic from September 1962 set the pattern, the vanguard of decline. Until this time there had been isolated, piecemeal closures as in Ringwood – Christchurch in 1935, the Gosport branch from Fareham, where passenger services ceased on 8 June 1953, the Meon Valley line between Fareham and Alton which also closed to passengers in February 1955, for example – closures that did little to affect the essential structure and fabric of railway services.

Early summer 1964 saw the next significant assault. As from 4 May that year the former Salisbury and Dorset Junction line from West Moors to Alderbury Junction, on the Romsey-Salisbury line – the route taken by cross-country services from Bournemouth to South Wales – closed to all traffic. On the same day, the local services that had operated from Bournemouth West to Brockenhurst via Wimborne and Ringwood were withdrawn; passenger services to the communities along this route were no more. Bereft of its former traffic and essential function, Bournemouth West closed on 4 October 1965; Boscombe station closed the same day.

Replacement of steam by diesel traction was not frenetic as on the Western Region, for example. The long-term intention had been electrification, which was achieved to Bournemouth on 10 July 1967. During the previous week, *The Bournemouth Belle* saw the last steam workings on Wednesday 5 July, when the 'down' service was headed by 'West Country' No 34024 *Tamar Valley* and the 'up' train by No 34036 *Westward Ho*. The last steam service to Waterloo, on 9 July was the 2.07 pm Weymouth-Waterloo which was headed by 'Merchant Navy' No 35030 *Elder Dempster Lines*. *The Bournemouth Belle* that day was headed by Class 47, Brush Type 4, No 1924. It handled the train in both directions. With it went the famous names – *Bournemouth Belle, Royal Wessex, Pines Express*. Electric services, backed up by colour light signalling, progressively implemented since the summer of 1966, also saw the end of the familiar and distinctive semaphore signalling, although this was something of a gradual and selective process.

Hindsight shows that 1967 brought the most obvious outward expression of change, but no-one could doubt that the previous five years were characterised, defined, by the process of transition. The railway system serving this distinctive part of the 'Sunny South Coast', as it stood in the late summer of 1967, was very different in character, emphasis and structure from that of the corresponding period in 1962. Five years of far-reaching fundamental change marked the decisive break with both the recent past, and with practices and traditions reaching back across the century. –